furniture care:

REPAIRING & RESTORING
chests & cabinets

furniture care:

REPAIRING & RESTORING
chests & cabinets

professional techniques to bring your furniture back to life

WILLIAM COOK

W. J. COOK & SONS

PHOTOGRAPHY BY **JOHN FREEMAN**

southwater

This edition is published by Southwater

Southwater is an imprint of Anness Publishing Ltd
Hermes House, 88–89 Blackfriars Road, London SE1 8HA
tel. 020 7401 2077; fax 020 7633 9499; www.southwaterbooks.com; info@anness.com

© Anness Publishing Ltd 2005

UK agent: The Manning Partnership Ltd, 6 The Old Dairy, Melcombe Road, Bath BA2 3LR;
tel. 01225 478444; fax 01225 478440; sales@manning-partnership.co.uk

UK distributor: Grantham Book Services Ltd, Isaac Newton Way, Alma Park Industrial Estate, Grantham,
Lincs NG31 9SD; tel. 01476 541080; fax 01476 541061; orders@gbs.tbs-ltd.co.uk

North American agent/distributor: National Book Network, 4501 Forbes Boulevard, Suite 200, Lanham,
MD 20706; tel. 301 459 3366; fax 301 429 5746; www.nbnbooks.com

Australian agent/distributor: Pan Macmillan Australia, Level 18, St Martins Tower, 31 Market St, Sydney,
NSW 2000; tel. 1300 135 113; fax 1300 135 103; customer.service@macmillan.com.au

New Zealand agent/distributor: David Bateman Ltd, 30 Tarndale Grove, Off Bush Road, Albany, Auckland;
tel. (09) 415 7664; fax (09) 415 8892

A CIP catalogue record for this book is available from the British Library.
Publisher: **Joanna Lorenz**
Editorial director: **Judith Simons**
Project editors: **Charlotte Berman, Lucy Doncaster and Claire Folkard**
Text editor: **Alison Bolus**
Designer: **Lisa Tai**
Photographer: **John Freeman**
Technical director: **Paul Lyon, W.J. Cook & Sons**
Editorial reader: **Richard McGinlay**
Production controller: **Claire Rae**

Previously published as part of a larger volume, *The Complete Guide to Repairing & Restoring Furniture*

1 3 5 7 9 10 8 6 4 2

PUBLISHER'S NOTE

The author and publisher have made every effort to ensure that all instructions contained in this book are accurate and that the safest
methods are recommended. The publisher and the author cannot accept liability for any resulting injury, damage or loss to persons or
property as a result of using any tools in this book or carrying out any of the techniques or projects. Before you begin any restoration task,
you should know how to use all your tools and equipment safely and be sure and confident about what you are doing.

CONTENTS

INTRODUCING CHEST AND CABINET RESTORATION

Whatever the date, period or style, at some point every chest and cabinet will need repair or restoration. At the very least, with the opening and closing of drawers, runners will be worn down and stops lost. In the past, repairs were often simply fashioned to make the piece serviceable, sometimes not even in the timber of the original. But with the burgeoning interest in antiques, today's chests and cabinets need skilled restoration.

Inherited chests and cabinets are highly valued now but were once considered just secondhand furniture. Blacksmiths' brackets were used for repairs and pieces were adapted according to fashion and usage. Legs were added, handles replaced and pieces reduced. Bun feet are a classic example. Fashionable during the late 17th century, they were replaced with the new style of bracket foot during the 18th century. The original bun feet absorbed moisture from stone floors laid directly on to earth foundations and rotted away.

Understanding the construction of the piece, including the techniques used during its period, is vital when restoring chests and cabinets. Equally important as employing the relevant restoration method is access to the correct tools, a suitable work environment and, when necessary, antique timbers to patch damaged areas. Before beginning any restoration project, it should be thought through, with potential problems analysed and best solutions realized. Approached incorrectly, the easiest of tasks can soon develop into a major undertaking. It makes no sense to begin gluing a chest or cabinet together only to discover that a special cramp or an extra pair of hands is needed. Equally, if a chest or cabinet must be knocked apart great care is needed to avoid further damage or hammer marks. Also important is the understanding of how and why a design developed. Increasingly research is needed to work out what was originally present but has since been lost or changed – for instance, galleries, mouldings or

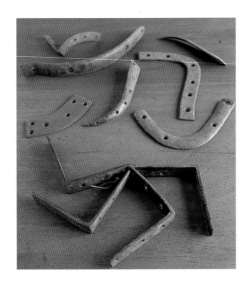

Above: *A selection of smith-made brackets, which were used to act as temporary strengtheners on loose furniture.*

Right: *This is a classic example of how furniture can be altered over the years as fashions change. The original bun feet on this late 17th-century chest were replaced with bracket versions sometime during the 18th century. Note also the addition of later 18th-century swan-necked handles.*

Above: *A George III tallboy sensitively restored so that the repairs blend seamlessly with the original workmanship.*

mounts may have been altered or replaced to suit the contemporary fashion. The aesthetics of a cabinet can be rebalanced just by the removal of a later addition and the correct replacement or by a chest being returned to its original height or proportions.

A huge responsibility lies upon the shoulders of the antique chair restorer. In front of him is a piece of history, often with a surface that has developed its unique qualities over centuries. This uniqueness can be lost in an instant if the restorer applies the wrong methods. It is this skill of knowing how and what to do – and in many cases what not to do – that is the difference between a competent restorer and an amateur. So if in doubt, always consult an experienced restorer. If considerately approached he is usually willing to offer advice and say if he thinks a project is too adventurous.

Those who can handle the tools of antique restoration correctly should consider further education. There are a number of college courses designed to train the student restorer. Some would say that before attendance the student

should already be trained and even qualified as a competent cabinet-maker., Unfortunately, in today's hectic lifestyle, it is not always possible to gain previous cabinet-making experience. Restoration courses can range from a few months to one, two or three years. It should be remembered that after the completion of any course the gulf between classroom and workshop practice is wide. Nothing will replace the hours spent at the bench, honing and developing one's skills and working with experienced restorers who have spent a lifetime learning their craft.

Another development to be aware of is the debate of restoration versus conservation. There now exist two schools of thought: one advocates that a piece should be restored and, with the use of old or breaker pieces of timber, returned to a state where the work is, as far as possible, unnoticeable; the other advocates that repairs should be carried out sympathetically but without blurring the line between old and new. While both sides have merit, from a commercial perspective, unobtrusive restoration wins the argument. Some techniques simply involve regluing loose joints and broken legs or attending to worn runners or lost stops, but the debate begins when a leg or a piece of veneer is lost.

As illustrated in this book, a requirement of any serious workshop is an adequate breaker store. This will consist of timbers dating from the 17th, 18th and 19th centuries, hopefully to match the colour, grain and texture of a piece under repair. A seamless repair is far more desirable than using new timber. Whatever their differences of opinion, both restorers and conservators would agree that any colour and patination the chest or cabinet has developed be left unaltered.

An understanding of colour and surface is vital because, while previously the restorer would pass the chest or cabinet to the polisher to perform any necessary colouring, polishing or waxing, it is now common to find a restorer acting as both

cabinet-maker and polisher. This dual role means that the restorer must have a large area of expertise and not only be able to colour in small repairs but also, when required, polish entire sets of chairs.

The importance of the restorer is increasing greatly as both the trade and public are buying more antique chests and cabinets that require attention before they can be sold or used. Additionally, the next generation inheriting chests and cabinets are realizing the value of their legacies and appreciating the skill and workmanship involved in their original construction. They know that their chests and cabinets must be well cared for and restored if they are to survive for future generations.

Those who are prepared to invest time in learning their craft thoroughly while building up their historical knowledge, not to mention their supplies of timber, and increasing their practical ability, can be assured of a rewarding and satisfying interest or career. It should be remembered though that, as with everything in life, what one puts in is what one takes out – and never more so than in the field of antique cabinet restoration.

Right: An early 19th-century linen press with good colour and patination. Both should be retained during restoration

HISTORY OF CHESTS AND CABINETS

Unlike chairs or tables, cabinets and chest of drawers have changed radically throughout their history. While their function has always been primarily for storage, in certain periods, particularly during the 18th century, they also became a symbol of the owner's wealth and position in society. As such, the chest of drawers was displayed in a prominent position in the main room of the house, the drawing room, and was known as a commode.

The modern chest of drawers evolved from the chest or coffer (the terms were interchangeable in medieval times). During the 15th century, when coffers first appeared in a form that would be recognizable today, furniture was a rare commodity. Even the largest hall's furniture would consist of little more than a large chair for the master of the house, stools for the rest of the household, a large table at which the household would dine, a cupboard and a coffer to store valuables, clothes and food.

The earliest coffers, dating from the late 13th century, were simply hollowed-out logs with the outsides squared off and the lids attached by raised peg hinges. The next advance was a coffer constructed from roughly hewn boards that were fixed together with wooden dowel pegs; shaping the taller ends formed simple feet.

They were made secure by crude iron strap hinges and locks. The obvious problem with this form of construction – especially as most of the wood used was unseasoned – was that the planks frequently split. Most decoration was fairly crude, although the earliest forms of carving are found as well as some paintwork. Some coffers, mainly those designed for travel, were bound in iron

Above: *The earliest coffers were little more than planks of oak nailed and held together with iron straps.*

Left: *By the 15th century, panel construction allowed more elaborate decoration.*

and covered with studded leather. These coffers, with their distinctive shape and rope handles at the ends, were known as trussing coffers, or standards.

The next major development, during the late 15th and early 16th centuries, was the framed or panel coffer. This, as the name suggests, was a coffer made up of an oak framework joined by mortise and tenons. The panels were simply fitted loose into grooves in the styles, rails and muntins, which allowed for shrinkage without the wood splitting. The more stable coffer gave the craftsman greater scope for decoration, and from this period onward many of the chests were highly carved. By the late 16th century, decorative inlays of bone and of wood such as holly or box are also found. Some of the earliest decorated coffers were carved with the linenfold pattern, which perhaps mimics the natural ripple in the wood. Carvings became more and more complex, and by the late 17th century not only were carved figures incorporated into the panels and uprights but also regional differences had begun to develop, each with their own distinctive style of manufacture and decoration.

During this period, with more people owning books (themselves a valuable commodity at the time), bookcases began to appear. At first they had solid panel doors, but by the late 17th century the finest examples had mirror plate or hand blown glass doors.

The first chest of any description, more commonly known as the mule chest, was in fact a coffer with a large drawer set at the bottom. It appeared during the late 16th century, but it was not until the 17th century that the chest of drawers in the form we recognize today actually developed.

The chest, still made in the majority in oak, rapidly changed its form. At first the drawers were made by simply nailing the softwood linings together and housing them on inset runners. Then finer linings were cut from quarter-sawn oak and joined with dovetails to aid strength and rigidity. The second half of the 17th century saw an increased use of

walnut and the introduction of veneers. The latter brought about a change in construction in cabinets and chests of drawers: where before they were made from solid oak or walnut, the carcass was now constructed from a softwood such as pine on to which was applied the decorative veneer. This was taken to an even greater extreme in France, where tortoiseshell and intricate brass inlays were being used by the royal cabinet-maker André-Charles Boulle (1642–1732). This was also used, but perhaps not to the same level, in England by the royal cabinet-maker Gerrit Jensen (fl.1680–1715), who is more commonly associated with the use of intricate seaweed marquetry.

With the use of veneer becoming more fashionable in the better houses, long-grain moulding was replaced with bolder cross-grain moulding, which gave a more decorative finish. It is interesting to note that it was due to economic rather than technical restrictions that the use of marquetry ceased in English furniture toward the end of the 17th century, although it continued to feature in French

Above: *A late 17th-century English chest of drawers showing the influence of the imported fashion of inlaid marquetry.*

and Italian furniture. In England, the use of decorative veneers once again came to the fore, supplemented with decorative herringbone bandings and inlay.

The late 17th century saw a number of structural changes to the chest and cabinet. A new method of allowing the drawers to slide in and out of the carcass was introduced: the previously side-hung drawer runners were replaced with runners applied to the drawer bottoms. The practice also emerged of raising the chest off its feet with the use of a low stand, itself often fitted with a drawer. While commonly found in either oak or walnut veneer, these pieces were sometimes, when made for the wealthiest of patrons, constructed in Europe and then transported to China to be lacquered. On their return they were placed on elaborate carved stands that would be silver gilded. The chest on stand, while continuing occasionally to be ▷

commissioned during the 18th century, was largely replaced by the tallboy, or chest on chest. As the name suggests, these were two chests, one on top of the other, which offered double the storage. The better examples would have canted corners, a secretaire interior or perhaps an inset sunburst to the base drawer.

The form of the chest of drawers and cabinet changed very little until around 1720, when mahogany imported from Cuba and Honduras began to be used in the manufacture of the finest pieces of furniture. With its dense grain and ease of working, mahogany ideally suited the needs of an emerging wealthy clientele who were demanding a wider diversity of furniture to house their ever-growing collections of valuable objects and expanding libraries. While the chest's primary function was still the storage of clothing, a new piece of furniture emerged from France – the commode.

The commode was grander and far more intricate than the simple chest, its place being in the drawing room under an imposing work of art and surrounded by fine objects collected from around the world. The leading makers and designers of the 18th century, such as Thomas Chippendale, published design and

pattern books for commodes and cabinets, which were subscribed to by all the leading members of the European aristocracy. Commodes and cabinets were constructed from the finest mahogany and decorated with elaborate carving. With the importation of exotic woods during the mid-18th century, combined with the desire for a lighter and more elegant look, marquetry decoration

Above: By the 18th century, the finest French commodes were often lacquered and embellished with fire-gilded mounts.

Left: This Georgian mahogany breakfront bookcase with drawers, possibly Chippendale, dates from around 1760.

re-emerged. Its revival was short-lived, as by the end of the century the chest was once again largely being consigned to the role of clothes storage, while bookcases and cabinets developed both in scale and variety to include secretaire drawers, opening cupboard bases and elaborate cornices and pediments.

During the early to mid-19th century, chests of drawers gradually became larger. In previous centuries, most people owned a very limited number of clothes, but now the emerging merchant classes had more changes of dress than before. Therefore larger, more utilitarian chests were required. To help keep the costs of manufacture down, making the chests more accessible to the new market, mahogany veneer was often used instead of solid wood. The ability to knife-cut rather than saw-cut the expensive imported mahogany facilitated the manufacture of a more affordable yet still desirable product.

The overall style and design of the chest and cabinet was to remain largely unaltered from the early 20th century onward, although they did undergo stylistic changes during the early part of the century with a cleaner, less elaborate style being favoured by the emerging designers of the Art Deco period.

CHEST CONSTRUCTION

The chest, be it 17th-, 18th- or 19th-century, consists of a series of drawers enclosed in a carcass. The drawers, depending on their date, will have to run on drawer runners. Chests vary in size from small bachelors' chests, often no larger than 75cm/30in wide, to chests so tall that the top drawers cannot be seen into. Their location was usually in the bedroom, but the finest commodes were prominantly displayed in the drawing room.

On mid-17th-century chests, drawer runners were often attached to the carcass sides and slotted into the side linings of the drawers. By the late 17th century, the runners were attached to the underside of the drawer. This meant that the weight was better dispersed and the runners could easily be replaced when worn.

To ensure that the drawers stopped neatly in the right place when pushed in, drawer stops were used. Like the runner, however, they were susceptible to wear and needed replacing from time to time. By the 18th century, dust boards were incorporated between the drawers. These helped to strengthen the carcass and enabled locks to be fitted on each drawer, if required.

The earlier chests of drawers, dating from the 16th to the mid-17th centuries, were generally made of solid wood and had long-grain mouldings. Some were decorated with carving or limited inlays.

With the arrival of veneers in the latter part of the 17th century, the carcass was usually made of softwood on to which walnut veneers or even marquetry were applied. The veneer was laid with quarter patterns embellished with herringbone inlay bandings. The use of long-grain mouldings was replaced with cross-grain mouldings, which, like the veneer, gave a far more decorative look. In France this went even further with elaborate brass boulle (buhl) inlays inset to tortoiseshell or ebony backgrounds.

By the early 18th century mahogany was once again being used in its solid form, with the use of veneer not returning until the importation of exotic timbers such as satinwood some 40 years later. The chest was further enhanced with decorative features such as canted corners, detailed carving, applied blind fret decoration or a brushing slide.

The feet would reflect the style of the time. Bun feet were the choice of the 17th century, giving way to the shaped bracket foot of the 18th century, and by the 19th century plinths were often used on bedroom chests. The changing fashions are often reflected in the hardware, and it is not unusual to find a chest that has had its handles changed a number of times.

Right: The basic construction of the chest of drawers varied little during the 18th and 19th centuries.

carcass style

carcass rail

linings

dovetail joints

bracket feet

top

dust boards

runner

stop

handle

escutcheon

base moulding

Tools, equipment and materials

The right tools, equipment and materials are the lifeblood of

any restorer. Often passed from generation to generation,

they must be cared for and used with the skill they deserve,

for without them even the most gifted of restorers will be

unable to undertake the most basic of restoration jobs.

CREATING A WORKSPACE

More often than not, financial limitations and space will dictate the location of a workshop. The most important piece of equipment in the workshop will be the bench, so it is important that any area under consideration should,

as a basic requirement, be able to house both you and the bench, as well as allowing space for the furniture being restored. You will also need to surround yourself with tools and machinery, so plan your work area carefully.

YOUR WORKBENCH

Once you have decided where to site your workbench, you will need to assess the various factors that are vital for good work.

The most important factor is the quality of light available. Natural light is ideal, so, if possible, position the bench directly under a window or skylight. Hang fluorescent strip lights above the workbench and, if you are intending to undertake any polishing work, make sure that normal lights are also available

(fluorescent light gives a false colour). Also paint the walls white to reflect, and so maximize, whatever light there is.

Rack your tools in an organized manner so that they are readily available. Keep groups of tools, such as hammers, saws or chisels, together for easy access. Keep tools that are not used daily, such as carving tools, carefully wrapped to protect their sharp edges, and stored neatly ready for use. Above all, keep the work area and bench clean and tidy.

Remember that most of your time will be spent standing at the workbench, so put blocks under it, if necessary, to set it at a height that is comfortable for you to work at. Also, if possible, opt for a wooden rather than a concrete floor, as concrete is very tiring on the feet and legs.

If space and funds permit, have two separate areas within the workshop: one for cabinet making and the other, in a dust-free area, for polishing. This dual use maximizes the available space.

An ideal workbench

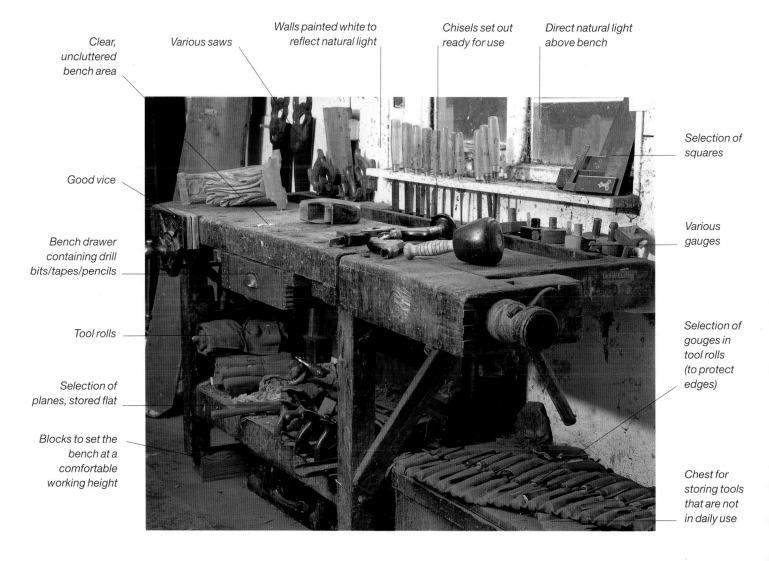

Clear, uncluttered bench area

Various saws

Walls painted white to reflect natural light

Chisels set out ready for use

Direct natural light above bench

Selection of squares

Good vice

Various gauges

Bench drawer containing drill bits/tapes/pencils

Tool rolls

Selection of gouges in tool rolls (to protect edges)

Selection of planes, stored flat

Blocks to set the bench at a comfortable working height

Chest for storing tools that are not in daily use

YOUR TOOLKIT

When restoring antique furniture, the best tools are, without doubt, those that were originally used in the 18th and 19th centuries. For a hobby restorer, modern tools are a suitable, and realistic, substitute, but anyone wishing to pursue a career in the field of furniture restoration should endeavour to build up as wide a collection of antique tools as possible. Such tools were made by craftsmen for craftsmen. The steel used then is still the best for holding a suitable cutting edge now, and the handles, made from box or rosewood, feel more comfortable to the hand than modern materials such as plastic. Often you will see numerous names stamped into the handle of an antique tool, indicating how it has passed through the hands of generations of craftsmen.

Old tools can be found in a number of places, ranging from specialized tool auctions or car boot sales, to local fêtes and classified advertisements in the local paper. If you are really lucky, you may have the opportunity to buy the tools and contents of the workshop of a retiring cabinet-maker. If this happens, beg or borrow the funds to buy the tools, since such events are rare indeed.

In the absence of antique tools, or while you are building up your collection, start your toolkit by buying modern equivalents, but be sure to buy the best quality that is available within your budget. Clamps are an exception to this rule, and modern sash, snap and G-clamps are fine. These are expensive pieces of equipment, so it is a good idea to buy a few whenever you can afford them.

Modern screwdrivers, saws and chisels can be purchased to begin with, and you can gradually replace them with older examples if you want. Some tools and equipment, such as spring clips, can be made in the workshop (see p.57).

Most cabinet-makers take a lifetime to build up their collection of tools, and almost all craftsmen will prefer to work with only their own tools, which, once purchased, should last a lifetime.

If you become interested in restoring then you may become an avid collector of tools yourself. Certainly, if you decide to take up restoring as a job, then building up your stock of tools and materials can be seen as an investment in your own future. Remember always to respect your tools, keeping them clean and sharp, and wrapping them safely whenever they are not in use.

Safety

The safety rules of a workshop are esentially those of common sense. Always remember that the workshop is potentially a dangerous area, so make sure that children cannot get in. Always handle sharp tools with care and replace them in their rack after use. Keep a regularly tested fire extinguisher close to hand and lock any flammable materials away in a fireproof cabinet. Keep the work area clean and tidy and sweep up all shavings at the end of the day. Good ventilation is important, especially when using stripper or any other chemicals. Make sure any stains or other liquids are kept in jars and clearly labelled. Wear suitable safety clothing as the job dictates. Tie back long hair, remove any dangling jewellery and always wear a long apron to protect your clothes.

Above: *A fire extinguisher is essential. Install a powder-filled fire extinguisher at every exit door.*

Above: *When using power tools likely to create a lot of dust or sparks, it is a good idea to wear a protective helmet.*

Left: *Basic safety equipment should include a first-aid kit, goggles, ear defenders, a filter mask , gloves and a disposable mask.*

SAWS AND MEASURING DEVICES

It is important that saws are kept in good condition because a sharp edge is essential, particularly when doing detailed work. Although modern power saws can take much of the effort out of sawing, and certainly have their place in a workshop, hand-held saws, such as the tenon saw, are invaluable for small-scale work. Measuring devices, including dividers, callipers and gauges, are the key to successful cabinet work, so look after them carefully.

SAWS

The three most commonly used saws in day-to-day restoration are the full tenon saw, the half-tenon saw and the dovetail saw, all of which have varying numbers of teeth per centimetre (inch). The more teeth per centimetre (inch), the finer the cut will be. Some of the finest cutting teeth are those of the fret and coping saws, designed for detailed shape work.

The large panel saw, used for cutting larger boards, comes with two teeth settings: the cross cut, designed to cut across the grain, and the ripsaw, designed to cut along the length of the grain. With the introduction of modern band saws and circular saws, large panel saws are used less frequently, but all workshops should have at least one of each type.

Saws will almost certainly be used on a daily basis and should be used only for the specific task for which they were designed. Using a fine dovetail saw for general work, for example, will damage the teeth and make it unsuitable for the finer work of cutting dovetails.

The saw is a precision cutting tool and should always be kept sharp and in good condition. While it is possible to sharpen the saw yourself, it is far better to send it to a professional saw doctor to have the teeth set and sharpened.

Left: *Three saws from a typical workshop, each with a different number of teeth per centimetre (inch). The more teeth a saw has, the finer the cut will be.*

Above: *An extensive range of reliable measuring tools is essential for the furniture restorer to carry out accurate work.*

When using a saw on a particularly difficult piece of wood, rub a little candle wax on the blade to help ease the cutting.

MEASURING DEVICES

"Measure twice, cut once" is an old cabinet-makers' saying, and it is as true today as it has always been. Accurate measuring is vital, since if the measuring is inaccurate then all the work that follows is wasted, at worst possibly leading to a ruined piece of valuable furniture, at best meaning you have to start all over again. Measuring tools include dividers, marking gauges, callipers, set (carpenter's) squares, sliding bevels and box rules, all of which are indispensable. Double-check every measurement and work from a face edge (the first edge cut and planed level, which is then used to take other measurements).

HAMMERS AND SCREWDRIVERS

Hammers, ranging from pin hammers for light work to heavier hammers for knocking apart furniture, are an essential part of any restoration work, as are the various types of mallet, particularly the carver's dummy, which is a very useful tool. A wide range of screwdrivers should also be kept to hand. Look out for examples with long and short shanks, which are useful in different situations. Be sure to keep the leading edge of a screwdriver sharp.

HAMMERS

The restorer will have two or three different types in the workshop, including the light pin hammer, the general cabinet hammer, which will be used on a daily basis, and a heavier hammer used to knock apart carcasses and drive in large nails. Hammers should never be used to hit another tool, such as a chisel – that is exclusively the role of the mallet.

When the face of a hammer becomes dirty and worn, file it flat then rub it lightly with fine-grade sandpaper to remove the dirt and score the surface. This enables the hammer to grip the head of the nail. This process, which is known as "dressing", will probably need to be done at least two or three times a month.

MALLETS

These were designed to be used against the handle of a tool such as a chisel or gouge. They come in different weights and shapes, and the greater the weight of the head, the more force it will exert. A good example of this is the carver's dummy, whose heavy lignum vitae head

Above: *Two traditional mallets – it is useful to have a selection in your workshop.*

ensures that a simple wrist action gives a very strong blow. It also means that the carver need not look at the mallet as it swings down, since its rounded head will always strike the tool being used, thus allowing the carver to concentrate fully on the work in hand.

Larger mallets are for roughing off, while lighter ones are for delicate work. The square-headed mallet is for general cabinet work and knocking apart, where a large hammer might bruise the wood.

SCREWDRIVERS

It is best to equip yourself with as wide a range of screwdrivers as possible. It is well worth spending a little time at car boot sales or trawling through second-hand shops in order to build a collection of traditional tools at a lower price than new ones. Old screwdrivers tend to have a longer shank, which gives better leverage. They also have handles made from box-wood or beech, which are kinder to the hand than plastic. Small screwdrivers with short shanks can be very useful for removing screws in awkward locations.

When buying an old screwdriver, check that the leading edge is straight and even. If it is worn or uneven, you will have to grind it flush, because a screwdriver that does not fit snugly into a screw-head slot can break the screw. Remember that a screwdriver is designed for removing and putting in screws and should never be used as a lever, which could damage the edge and bend the shank.

Below: *A selection of old screwdrivers with shanks of varying lengths.*

Holding a hammer

1 *When using a hammer, the most common mistake is to hold it half way down the handle in the belief that this allows more control and accuracy. In fact, it has the opposite effect.*

2 *The correct way to hold the hammer is at the end of its handle, which gives much better balance and control. When using a hammer, make several medium blows rather than trying to drive the nail home first time.*

SMOOTHING TOOLS AND CLAMPS

There are many different types of planes and clamps used in restoration work, and modern tools are very similar to their traditional counterparts. Some planes are fitted with their own guide fences and others with changeable blades, while moulding planes have specially shaped bases and blades for detailed shaping work. Different clamps, like planes, are designed for particular tasks and it is advisable to build up as wide a selection as possible.

PLANES

The earliest planes were made with wood bodies, but during the 18th and 19th centuries the metal-bodied plane took over, although the moulding planes remained wooden.

There are various examples of planes, each suited to a particular role, including the utilitarian jack plane, the smoothing plane, and the smaller block-and-shoulder plane for more intricate work. There are also specialized planes, such as moulding planes, with their specially shaped bases and blades, which are designed to cut the waist, base and other mouldings found on carcass furniture. However, the modern router, with its wide range of shaped cutters, has largely taken over this role. Although the spokeshave does not look like a plane, it is classed as one because it works along the same principle.

The blade of any plane is designed to cut the wood cleanly without tearing the grain, and so it is important that it is always kept sharp. When the blade is sharp and the plane is used correctly, it should made a wonderful slicing sound as it cuts through the wood.

SCRAPERS

The cabinet scraper, which is basically a piece of metal with a burred edge, is designed to clean up surfaces and remove any plane marks prior to sanding.

The most frequently used scraper will be a rectangular one for shaped mouldings, but tailor-made scrapers are also useful. The most common example is the French curve, which is shaped like a kidney and should be able to scrape any concave area.

Scrapers should always be used sharp and should produce shavings, not dust. To sharpen a scraper, you should draw a hard piece of rounded metal, such as the shank of a screwdriver, across the edge. This produces a burr, which is needed to cut the wood.

SANDING EQUIPMENT

The earliest types of sandpaper were, in fact, made from sharkskin, known as shagreen. It was dried and used very much in the same way as sandpaper is today. This was followed by the use of ground glass or sand, which was stuck to paper, and it is from this that the terms "glasspaper" and "sandpaper" are derived.

Nowadays there are many abrasive papers available, including silicon carbide, aluminium oxide and garnet paper, but the term "sandpaper" is still commonly used to describe them all. These papers are available in a number of different grits, or grades, with the most commonly used grits in the workshop ranging from 80 (the coarsest) to 320 (the finest).

Sandpaper is rarely used on its own but is wrapped around sanding blocks of cork or wood. If a specific moulding has to be sanded, you will need to make a shaped piece of wood (overloe) that matches the profile of the moulding, so that it can be sanded without having its shape altered. Over the years, the restorer will build up a wide selection of tailor-made overloes.

When you start sandpapering a piece of work, begin with the coarsest grade and work up through the grades to the finest. Wetting the wood between each grade, and allowing it to dry before you start with the next grade, will give a smoother finish. Also, if you intend to apply a water stain, this inter-grade wetting process will make sure that the grain does not rise at the staining stage.

Above: *A selection of planes showing some of the variety of shapes and materials used in their construction.*

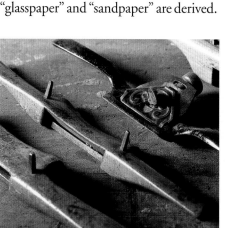

Above: *The spokeshave is a cross between a plane and a scraper, and is a very versatile tool for shaping wood.*

Above: *Overloes are specially shaped wooden blocks that are used with sandpaper to smooth the profile of a moulding.*

CLAMPS

These tools come in a wide variety of styles, each suited to a particular role. The most common types are the long sash clamp, the G-clamp, which comes in different sizes, the band clamp, the snap clamp and the spring clip (see p.57). Modern clamps are similar to traditional ones, and although they are fairly expensive to buy, it is best to have as wide a range as possible.

When working with clamps, always use clamping blocks to prevent bruising and the appearance of "hoof" marks on the wood. Also, never over-tighten a clamp: the pressure it exerts can cause structural damage to delicate pieces.

When gluing up a complex job, it is a good idea to have a "dry" run beforehand, working out which clamps will be used and in which order. Spending a little time doing this may prevent problems later on when the glue has been applied and is setting. It also means that you will have everything you need to hand and will feel confident about starting the work.

Above: *A wide selection of modern and traditional clamps, including G-clamps and sash clamps, are essential for many types of restoration work.*

Making a band clamp

While most clamps can be bought, the steel band clamp is unique in that it is workshop made and tailored to a particular job in hand. Its role is to clamp an oval or round, creating an equal pressure around the circumference.

You will need a small block of hardwood, a steel band (as used for binding building materials), small screws and a clamp.

1 *Cut two lengths of the steel band to a length slightly shorter than the frame's circumference and punch two pilot holes into each end of them.*

2 *Using a metal bit, drill two small holes through the pilot holes. Be sure to place a scrap block of wood on the bench or worktop to protect it.*

3 *Use a countersink drill bit to countersink the two holes previously drilled. This will make sure that the screw heads are level with the band.*

4 *After marking the shape of the frame on the hardwood, use a band saw to cut the concave profile. Cut the block in half.*

5 *Screw the two lengths of steel band to the shaped side of the hardwood, making sure that the countersunk hole side of the band is used.*

6 *Finish by filing the screw heads flush with the metal band, this will make sure that no unnecessary scratching or marking occurs.*

7 *The band clamp in use. The hardwood blocks are clamped together to create the tension.*

CHISELS AND CARVING TOOLS

All these implements have their own jobs, which involve paring away wood in one form or another, but one rule applicable to all is to keep their edges sharp so that they can cut through wood and not tear the grain. If you are interested in carving, you will start to amass a large collection of tools, since each has its own specific function. In general, old examples tend to keep their edge longer than modern versions, due to the better-quality steel.

CHISELS

The cabinet-maker or restorer will have three main types of chisel to hand on the workbench. These are the paring chisel, the mortise chisel and the firmer chisel. Within these groupings there should be a range of widths suitable for any task.

The paring chisel, with its bevelled edges and long blade, is primarily used for paring, levelling and chamfering. It is designed for hand-use only and should never be struck with a mallet.

The mortise chisel, as its name suggests, is used to cut out mortises, and for this reason its blade is noticeably thicker than that of both the paring and firmer chisels. The thickness of the blade means that it can withstand a heavy blow from a mallet and a certain amount of leverage when removing the waste wood from a mortise.

The firmer chisel, with its shorter, thicker blade without a bevelled side, is designed for heavier work and can be used in conjunction with a suitable mallet.

CARVING TOOLS

The carver is one of the most skilled craftspeople in the field of antique restoration. The skill of carving is similar to that of a painter, except that the carver's medium is wood and the end results are three-dimensional.

The required tools, which can number into the thousands, are known individually for their suitabilities and strengths, and before undertaking a carving project the carver will select the required implements and sharpen them. Indeed, depending on the hardness of the wood, it is not unknown for a carver to resharpen a blade every few minutes during carving work.

Small carving tools are essential for detailed and intricate work. They provide much greater control of the task in hand, allowing the carver to remove small slivers of wood with the minimum of effort.

There are numerous types of carving tools, including scrolls, which set out the shape of the carving; V- or parting tools, which produce long sweeps; grounders,

Above: *While gradually building up a collection of antique tools, which you can find in second-hand shops, it is a good idea to purchase modern equivalents too.*

which remove the background waste; veiners, which carve the fine details, such as flowers, leaves, etc; and fish tails, which, like the grounders, help to remove unwanted wood.

While this procedure may seem very complicated, it is worth noting that the complexity and intricacy of much of the work means that it takes several years for a carver to reach full potential.

Each carving project can often take hundreds of hours of painstaking work, and, aside from patience, the main skill a potential carver needs to learn is the ability to be able to study an existing carving closely and to mimic exactly the hand in which it was originally carved. The real test of the master carver is to restore carving to the extent that the new work blends in seamlessly with the original detail.

Left: *A selection of chisels, gouges and bradawls (for making fine pilot holes) will be used on a daily basis.*

Left: *A small selection of the many hundreds of carving tools required by the master carver.*

Above: *A carver's vice allows free and easy access to any carved piece held in it.*

Sharpening a chisel

Some of the tools most used by the cabinet-maker or furniture restorer are the various chisels. These are used to pare, level and shape the wood. It is vital that the chisels are kept sharp at all times, as failure to do so will result in them tearing the grain rather than slicing through the wood. When a chisel loses its edge, the process of re-honing takes only a few minutes, and the procedure is very simple.

1 *Using a grinding wheel and selecting the finest grade of the two stones, offer the chisel at an angle of approximately 25–30 degrees. Remove the bevel as soon as it is flat, otherwise the chisel's length will be shortened too much and its working life substantially reduced.*

2 *Lightly lubricate an oil stone with a fine oil, then draw the chisel repeatedly along the stone at an angle of 30–35 degrees. This will produce the cutting edge.*

3 *Turn the chisel over and lay it flat down on the stone. Rub it back and forth two or three times. This process, known as "backing off", will weaken the burr that has built up. Strop the chisel on a piece of leather, which should remove the burr.*

4 *Finally, use your newly sharpened chisel to cut a slither off a piece of wood. This will check for sharpness as well as removing the burr, should it not have come off on the leather strop.*

5 *The illustration shows how the finished edge should look if the chisel has been sharpened correctly.*

TURNING TOOLS

Since medieval times, turning has been used in the construction of furniture. While lathes have changed with the times – the earliest examples were human-powered – the basic techniques and principles used by the early bodgers (travelling lathe craftsmen) have remained much the same as they are today. Likewise, the tools used in modern workshops would still be recognizable to the turner of centuries past.

The tools of the turner are divided into measuring and turning tools. It is vital that accuracy is maintained, and this is done with the aid of the measuring tools: dividers to measure length and width and callipers to measure external or internal dimensions. Both take measurements from a template (pattern) and can be used easily when the lathe is in operation.

The turning tools, which have long blades and long handles to counteract the force of the lathe, are divided into four groups. First there are the gouges, which are used to rough off the wood to an approximate cylinder. Next are the skew chisels, used to refine the shape of the cylinder to its final form. The scrapers are used to make the grooves and turnings, and finally the parting tools are used to form long trenches and part the turnings from the waste wood.

Due to the stresses imposed on the tools they should be kept sharp and constantly checked for any possible stress fractures. This is one of the occasions when it is preferable for the restorer to use modern tools rather than their antique

equivalents. This is because the latter may have developed stress factors in their blades or faults in their handles, which, if fractured during application, could cause serious injury to the turner. It is also important, therefore, to make sure that the tools are always used correctly. Due to the potential risks involved when using a

Above: *A wide selection of measuring and turning tools is necessary to ensure that all turned work is accurate.*

lathe, it is essential to take an approved instructional course in turning before beginning lathe work (see Further Information, p.93).

Left: *The tap and die is a turning tool that is at the opposite end of the spectrum to high-speed lathes.*

Right: *Turning tools are distinctively different from woodworking chisels.*

Cutting a male screw thread

When turning and cutting a new thread, it is important to make sure that both male and female parts are of a corresponding size. As dies (internally threaded tools for cutting male threads) and screw taps (threaded steel cylinders for cutting female threads) exist in corresponding pairs, a match should be found. Remember that once you have started cutting, you must continue working until the thread is finished; stopping and starting will mean that you will not get a perfect match.

1 *Select and cut a piece of wood that is slightly larger in width than the diameter of the thread that is being replaced.*

2 *Turn the wood with a large gouge. Measure the size of the die housing using callipers, then compare this measurement to the size of the turned wood.*

3 *Turn the column to the final diameter required, checking the measurements with the callipers as you work.*

4 *Place the turned column in the vice and, using a sharp chisel, cut a leading edge in the column. This will aid the beginning of the thread cutting.*

5 *Place the die, which has an inset cutting blade, on top of the turned column. Start turning it in a clockwise direction to cut the thread.*

6 *Keeping the die level, follow the technique of one full rotation clockwise followed by one half rotation counterclockwise. This clears the blade of shavings.*

7 *Continue all the way to the base and then remove the die. Remove the wood column and cut it to the required length.*

Cutting a female screw thread

A corresponding female thread now needs to be cut to match the male thread. Should the female and male threads be of different sizes, a solution is to plug the female thread with a suitable piece of wood and then recut the female wood to a size to correspond with the male thread.

1 *Place a piece of wood in a vice. Drill a corresponding hole into it of compatible size to the turned male thread, then pare a leading edge on the hole with a sharp chisel.*

2 *Grip the screw tap in the vice and place the leading edge on top of it. Turn the piece of wood one complete turn clockwise followed by a half turn counterclockwise.*

3 *When completed, the male and female parts should fit snuggly together and the thread should work with ease.*

MACHINERY

While antique restoration is traditionally a craft that relies on hand-held tools, the use of machinery can, in certain cases, make life much easier. It was the mass introduction of mechanized tools during the 19th century that radically altered furniture production. Although they can never replace the trained craftsman, the new generation of hand-held power tools available today will certainly save you many valuable hours in the workshop.

The use of heavy machinery in the restoration workshop is fairly limited. In fact, not many restoration workshops will have the space for a fully fitted machine shop, especially as the heavier types often require three-phase electricity supplies. (This involves installing a unit to boost the power from single to three phase, and is usually needed only in commercial workshops.) However, the inclusion of certain heavy machines can make life much easier, and two invaluable machines are the band saw and the lathe.

Hand-held machine tools, such as an electric or cordless drill, jigsaw and router, are a great help, and you should stock as wide a range of router cutters as possible. You could also buy a router bench, which extends the possibilities of the router. As finances and space allow, you can buy extra machinery, such as circular saws, thickness planers and pillar drills.

While these tools will not be used on a daily basis, they can save hours of effort when they are required. As with all machinery, it is vital that you obtain the correct training before using them (see Further Information, p.93) and that you always carefully follow the safety instructions.

BAND SAW
The band saw's blade is a flexible length of steel that runs in a continuous loop. It is ideal for cutting curves and angles or for trimming strips from wider pieces. Its limitations are governed by the depth of the sawbed and the thickness of the blade. Never apply undue pressure to the blade, as this will damage it or the guiding rollers and cause it to snap.

As a general rule, allow the saw to cut at its own speed. Any excessive force will be indicated by the driving motors straining and starting to slow down.

band saw

lathe

LATHE
The lathe allows you to accomplish a wide variety of tasks, ranging from the turning of legs, bobbins, bead mouldings and spindles to the copying of handles and decorative roundels or paterae.

Due to the speed and torque at which lathes operate, a lathe with a heavy cast body is ideal for restoration work, as this will counter any vibration. It is essential to take an approved instructional course in lathe work before you start using one as misuse can result in serious injury.

router

router bench

jigsaw

electric drill

cordless drill

ROUTER

The router is an extremely versatile hand tool. Its shaped cutter rotates at high speeds and will, if used correctly, give a clean, even cut. It can also be used with a guide fence or depth stop, and the range of cutters available is immense. Care should be taken in its use: no loose clothing should be worn, hair should be tied back and eye protection should be worn.

ROUTER BENCH

The router bench allows the router to be mounted upside down and so converted into a spindle moulder. The bench should always be used with guide fences and safety guards. The bench can often be dismantled, allowing for convenient storage when not in use.

POWER DRILLS

Cordless and electric drills are both ideal machines for workshop use. While you may sometimes require the use of a more traditional hand drill, such as when undertaking delicate work that may need to be executed one turn of the drill bit at a time, a power drill is one of the few modern tools that is preferred over the old version.

Always buy the best model possible and, in the case of a cordless drill, always have the spare battery on charge ready to be changed over. These drills can also be used with screwdriver heads, although this would, of course, be for more general use and not for fine antique work, since the brass and steel antique screw heads would break if a power drill were used on them. Both types of drill can be used with a variety of bits and will accomplish a multitude of tasks. A drill stand can also be purchased to allow the drill to be used as a pillar drill.

JIGSAW

The jigsaw has a blade with a rise and fall action that cuts through sheet wood with ease. While it is not suitable for fine work, it is ideal for roughing out or cutting shaped templates (patterns) when the pieces are too large to fit into a band saw. Remember that the blade passes through the wood and continues to cut below, so care should be taken when using this tool.

COLLECTING AND STORING WOOD

A supply of suitable wood is an essential aspect of a restorer's workshop, and different kinds must be sourced, collected and properly stored. To the casual observer, such a collection of pieces of wood, salvaged from previous centuries of furniture making, may seem little more than firewood, but to the antique furniture restorer they are a priceless commodity, as without them his or her task would be impossible to undertake.

The aim of every restorer is, wherever possible, to restore a piece of furniture without trace. To do this requires the use of old surface woods and veneers that match the original as closely as possible in colour and grain. Also, when missing mouldings have to be remade, the material used must be of the same type as the original in order to make a good repair.

Two woods in constant demand by restorers are Cuban and Honduras mahogany, which, during the 18th century, were the woods of choice for furniture making. Both are now nearly impossible to buy from any wood merchant, and so any old examples found must be bought and put away until needed. This shows the vital importance of the restorer's "breaker store".

The breaker store, as the name so graphically describes, is a collection of pieces of antique furniture that have been bought not to be restored but to be carefully knocked apart, sorted into the various woods and stacked away for future reuse in the restoration of better pieces. Such an example might be a collection of quarter-sawn oak drawer sides, waiting to be used in the repair or replacement of a missing drawer, or perhaps an old Cuban mahogany table leaf, long ago separated from its table, waiting to be used in the making of a missing bracket foot or to be reshaped with a moulding plane to replace a missing section of top moulding.

The source of breakers is endless, and no opportunity should be missed to scour junk shops, local auctions or even skips. An old Victorian chest bought for very little indeed could provide enough oak linings, Cuban mahogany and even old locks to pay for itself many times over. Building a comprehensive breaker store can be a lifetime's work, and a useful tip to keep a store expanding is that every time some wood is used from the store, it should be replaced with more wood than was taken out. Indeed, it is a prerequisite for application to the antique restorers' most senior trade organization, The British Antique Furniture Restorers' Association (BAFRA), that the applicant is able to demonstrate the active building-up of a collection of breakers.

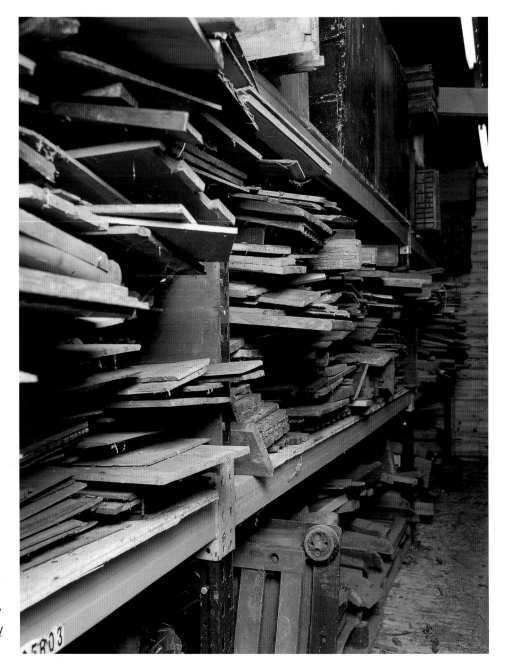

Right: A well-stocked and logically arranged breaker store will supply a restorer with wood to match virtually any restoration project.

The breaker store should be racked and labelled and the woods stored in the various marked sections. This saves both time and effort when searching for a particular piece and enables the restorer to see which, if any, types of veneer are running low or are not represented at all.

Any veneers should be removed from their wood core (see p.28) and stored separately in a veneer store. Any nails and screws should also be removed, partly for potential reuse if they are in good condition and partly as a method of preventing any unnecessary scratching from occurring. The store should be kept dry but not overly so, as excessive heat will cause the woods to warp and split, causing as many problems as dampness.

While the majority of woods will be old, if an opportunity arises it is a good idea to buy some modern woods, such as walnut, yew or oak for renovating country-made pieces. These should then be professionally cut into boards, stacked so that air can circulate freely between them and allowed to dry and season naturally under cover.

If, however, space will not allow this storage, and modern wood has to be purchased when needed, remember that it is always better to buy air-dried rather than kiln-dried wood, as the former will be more stable in the long term.

To the untrained eye, a restorer's breaker store may look like a confused jumble of wood. The owner, however, will know all the stock that is there, even wood that was acquired years ago. When a particular grain or surface is needed, the restorer should be able to locate it almost immediately, recalling it from the day it was placed there. Next to tools, an extensive and expanding supply of breakers is one of the most important considerations for a furniture restorer.

Below: *An example of the numerous repairs for which the components of a breaker chest can be used.*

Veneer used for patching small areas of damaged or missing veneer

Solid mahogany sides used for making bracket feet, mouldings, etc

Handles and locks used as replacements for missing ones

Oak drawer sides used for replacement sides or damaged drawers

Old surface pine from carcass used for patching old surfaces, etc

COLLECTING AND STORING VENEERS

While early furniture was made using solid wood, by the late 17th century the use of veneer was becoming more widespread. Originally cut by saw, by the latter part of the 19th century thinner (and therefore cheaper) veneers were cut by peeling the log, a technique known as "knife cut", which increased their use still further. Whenever possible, a comprehensive store of used and new veneer should be stocked.

Veneers, like breakers (see p.26), are an important commodity for any serious-minded restorer. While good veneer merchants will hold a comprehensive stock of various cuts of veneer, it is still a good idea for the restorer, wherever possible, to compile a separate store in a shed or unused room. This veneer store should include not only new veneers, which may be bought in bundles, often held together with string, but also old surface veneers, which may have been removed from breakers.

With time, the colour of certain woods can alter greatly from their original colour, and for this reason the furniture restorer should aim to collect as wide a range of old surface veneers as possible.

Left: *A selection of bandings and stringings, which are often used in veneer work, are useful. They can be purchased from good veneer merchants.*

Before being stored, old surface veneers will need to be removed from their core. A damp cloth is placed on top of the veneer and is then heated with an iron. The resulting steam softens the original animal glue, allowing the veneer to be gently eased off. This is done by sliding a flat-bladed knife between the veneer and the core. The old glue should be washed from the back of the veneer with hot water while it is still sticky.

The veneer should then be placed between two sheets of paper and have pressure applied to it. A hand veneer press is ideal for this, but alternatively the veneer can be placed between two flat pieces of wood with weights placed on top. This will allow the veneer to dry flat.

When the veneer is dry, it can be sorted with any other new pieces and then placed in the veneer store. Long lengths should be stored flat on slatted wood shelving, which allows the air to circulate freely. Smaller pieces, which can be used to repair

Left: *Any veneer store should be racked to allow the veneers to lie flat and be easily and quickly identified.*

cross bandings or inlays, can be placed in shoe boxes. The storage shed or room should not be allowed to become too dry, because this will cause the veneers to shrink and split. If possible, a slightly damp and cool atmosphere is best, because this allows the veneers to remain malleable. Laying cardboard on top of the veneer will also stop it becoming too dry and brittle.

Selecting a particular veneer from the store is a task best carried out by two people, one at each end of the veneer bundles, so that they can turn the bundles evenly as they search for the exact match. This method should prevent any unnecessary damage to the bundles. If, however, a veneer develops a split that starts to travel up its length, secure this with a piece of brown parcel tape.

When a piece of veneer has been removed from a shelf, the remaining pieces should be replaced in the same order as they were originally stacked. Failure to do so could result in different veneers being stacked together, which would then make selecting a particular veneer much harder in the future.

COLOUR AND PATINATION

Without doubt, the two most important aspects to any antique furniture are those of colour and patination. People often think that the two are the same, but in fact both are different, as each term refers to a different aspect of the finish found in antique furniture. It is the glorious colour and surface patination that furniture develops that the buyer and collector both seek. And their presence, or at times their absence, can radically alter the value of a particular piece.

Colour

The colour of a piece is found in the actual surface of the wood. This surface area illustrates how the wood has reacted over the years as many generations of natural light have affected its surface. It is interesting that for numerous reasons two pieces of the same wood, such as Cuban mahogany, can react in different ways. This can depend on the amount of light a piece has been exposed to or how dense a particular grain is. Also, a solid rounded piece, such as a chair upright, will react differently to a flat area, such as a chest top. Veneer will also change its appearance in a different way to a piece of solid wood.

Different woods can also be changed quite markedly over time, for instance kingwood and rosewood are both very purple when first cut and polished, but become a golden colour after many years of exposure. The change in mahogany, which when first polished has a very red tone, ranges from dark nutty brown to light honey colour. It is this variation that makes each piece of antique furniture unique. Unfortunately, this colour can easily be ruined by over-zealous cleaning, which allows chemicals to alter the tones, colours and hues of the wood. It is worth remembering that once altered, the original colour cannot be returned.

Patination

The term patination can best be described as the history of a piece mirrored in its surface colour and shine. Technically, it is caused by generations of oxidation of the polished surface, combined with a build-

Above and below: *These photographs illustrate the inner and outer surface of an 18th-century tea table. The inner surface, which has spent its lifetime closed and protected from the effects of light, has kept the original red colour (top). In contrast, the top of the table has mellowed and, after generations of waxing, has developed a magnificent patinated surface (below). This is an example of mahogany colour and patination at its best.*

up of furniture waxes, natural grease and dust. Its appearance can be altered by many factors, including sunlight, the amount of waxing a piece has received in its lifetime, whether any solvents have been applied and the type of finish originally used when the piece was made. For example, the patination found on a piece of mid-18th-century mahogany, which would have been polished with oil, varies greatly from that found on an early 18th-century piece of walnut, which would have been finished with varnish and wax. While good patination is often present on good pieces of furniture, truly great patination is rare. When it is present, therefore, every effort should be made to maintain it.

POLISHES AND GLUES

One of the most attractive features of antique furniture is its distinctive grain patterns. It is the application of polish and waxes that, while helping to protect, feed and nourish the wood, also enhances its appearance.

The polishes and techniques used today are nearly identical to those used for generations before, although the restorers of old would have had to make their own polish recipes as well as making all their own glues.

POLISHES

Ever since wooden furniture was first made, its grain has been sealed in one way or another. Waxes were used to burnish the surface, and, during the 17th century, varnishes were applied that helped to protect and enhance the wood. During the 19th century, a new technique was adopted that resulted in a shellac polish, made from the shells of lac beetles, being applied with a cotton and linen pad known as a rubber (see pp.49–50). This sealed the grain, protected the wood and brought out the pattern and figure of popular imported woods such as mahogany, satinwood and rosewood.

The polisher's basic requirements are few. The equipment involves wadding (batting) and linen or other lint-free cloth for making rubbers, a selection of various grades of wire (steel) wool, as well as a wide selection of various brushes and some mutton cloth for buffing surfaces.

The polisher's materials include shellac polish, which can be bought in either liquid form or as shellac flakes to be

mixed with spirit (alcohol), and is kept in a glass or plastic bottle. Various coloured pigments to be mixed with water or spirit are needed for tinting or colouring repairs, and stopping waxes, again in various shades, are also needed. The final material is methylated spirits (methyl alcohol), which should be stored in a fire-proof cabinet. All the above equipment and materials can be obtained from a good trade supplier.

One of the main attractions of an antique piece of furniture is its colour and, hopefully, its patinated surface, so great care should be taken whenever polish is applied. The skill of the polisher is to revive a surface by gently removing the perished layers and then rebuilding the surface layer by layer. Work on small areas should be kept as localized as possible so as not to affect the surrounding areas.

Above: *Brushes, polishes and stains are needed for nearly every restoration job. Keep a good selection to hand.*

Patience and practice are therefore the watchwords. A good eye for colour is also needed to ensure that patches and repairs blend in with the surroundings areas. They should be practically invisible. It is also essential to have an understanding of traditional techniques and materials and to know when to clean a piece and when it is better to leave it alone. Over-zealous cleaning will not only spoil the aesthetic appearance but will almost certainly devalue the piece considerably.

Professionally, a polisher may take many years to learn the craft, and, without doubt, the polisher's role in a workshop is every bit as important as that of the cabinet-maker or restorer.

Above: *Rubbers should be kept in an air-tight jar or tin to stop them drying out.*

GLUES

Until the 15th and early 16th centuries, very little glue was used in the manufacture of furniture. Instead, the joints were held together with pegs or crude, hand-made clout nails. By the 17th century, however, as furniture construction became more complex and designs and styles more adventurous, animal glues were being employed in furniture making.

While new adhesives have been developed over the years, animal glues are still the most frequently used glues in furniture restoration. The sight and smell of the glue pot in any workshop is the same today as it was in the 17th, 18th and 19th centuries, and putting it on the fire or hot plate is still the apprentice's first task every morning.

Three main types of glue are used in the modern workshop: animal glue, PVA (white) glue and cascamite. Each has its own role and will be selected according to the nature of the required join.

Animal glue

This glue is made today as it has been for the last 300 years: animal feet and skin are boiled and the resulting liquid is poured into cold water, causing it to crystallize and form small pearls. These pearls can then be mixed with water and allowed to soak overnight, before being heated in a special glue pot to melt them.

Above: *Animal glue is applied hot, using a bristle brush.*

Above: *The three most commonly used glues today (clockwise from top): animal glue, PVA (white) glue and cascamite.*

The glue pot (or gesso kettle) is an iron bain-marie pot with an inner reservoir of hot water. The pot is put on a fire or hotplate until the water boils, and it is then allowed to simmer gently, melting the glue ready for use. A top crust will appear and should be scraped off prior to use.

Great care should be taken not to allow the hot-water reservoir to boil dry. Should this happen, the glue will become too hot and its adhesive qualities will be lost. The remaining glue will then have to be discarded and a new batch prepared.

At the end of each day, the glue pot is taken off the heat and set aside until the next day, when it is simply reheated and the glue reused. A pot of glue could be cooled and then reheated day after day, but it is good workshop practice to make a fresh batch of animal glue every week.

Animal glue is ideal for furniture restoration because it allows a certain flexibility in the joints, it can be removed with hot water or spirit (alcohol) and it sets as soon as it has cooled. It can also be watered down to make a size for use on veneers and surfaces when a piece of furniture needs re-veneering.

The disadvantages of animal glue, however, are that it is affected by extremes of heat and cold and that a sharp blow to a joint will cause it to lose its adhesion. If such a break happens, the joint has to be taken apart, cleaned and reglued. Despite these disadvantages, however, no serious workshop would be without its glue pot.

Above: *Animal glues are heated prior to use in an iron bain-marie pot. The water reservoir should not be allowed to boil dry.*

PVA glue

Another frequently used glue is the more modern polyvinylacetate, or PVA (white), glue. It is bought in liquid form, is easy to use, needs no pre-application preparation and is unaffected by either extreme of temperature. The joint or two surfaces being joined must be brought under pressure when the glue (which is non-reversible) is applied.

When it is either impractical to have a glue pot simmering away all day, or when you are doing a small restoration job that simply does not warrant the time involved in preparing animal glue, versatile and simple-to-use PVA is the ideal workshop adhesive.

Cascamite

For projects needing an adhesive that will help to hold a shape or form, an ideal glue is urea-formaldehyde resin, or cascamite as it is more commonly known. This comes in a powder form and is mixed with water to a creamy paste. Once the glue has been applied, the two surfaces being joined should be brought under pressure with suitable clamps.

Cascamite is a versatile glue: its natural white colour can be disguised by adding coloured pigments to it, and some types are waterproof, which can be useful. The disadvantage, however, is that it is very brittle when set, making it totally unsuitable for joints, because just a knock could shatter the glue bond.

GILT AND STAINS

Gilding and staining are both methods of enhancing and disguising wood to give a better appearance. While stains are used in the main by the restorer to disguise repairs it should be remembered that during the 17th and 18th centuries inferior woods were often stained to give them the appearance of more exotic and expensive ones; for example pearwood was stained black to resemble the more sought after and expensive ebony.

GILT

The use of gilt to decorate and highlight furniture has been a part of furniture making for centuries. The two techniques used are those of oil and water gilding, each of which gives a distinctive look. Some specialist materials and equipment are needed, but the most important ingredients that the gilder requires are patience and skill.

Gesso is a mixture of powdered chalk, rabbit-skin glue and boiled linseed melted in a gesso kettle, and it is used to build up the surface before gilding. A few layers can give a thick, even coat. It can have sand mixed in with it for a textured finish.

Bole is a mixture of clay and water that is available in red, white or blue and is used to form the next layer in the gilding process. Once this is dry, a size of alcohol, rabbit-skin glue and water is applied. The surface is now ready for the gold leaf to be laid gently in place.

The gold used in gilding has been rolled on machine rollers and then hand-hammered into leaves of varying levels of

Above: *During the 17th and 18th centuries metalware on the finest pieces was occasionally fire gilded.*

fineness. It can be bought in a number of different grades, depending on the carat.

Agates are used to pull together joins between the leaves and for burnishing. Originally made from dog's teeth (they are also known as "dog-tooth agates"), they are now made from synthetic materials.

Water gilding

Gold leaf cannot simply be laid on to bare wood when water gilding. Bases of gesso and then bole must be applied first, and then the gilt can be laid, evened and finally distressed.

Right: *The tools of the gilder have remained basically the same through the centuries, although modern plastics are now replacing dog teeth.*

STAINS

The majority of coloured stains are either water- or spirit- (alcohol-) based, although on rare occasions a slow-drying, oil-based stain may be used. They are used to colour in repairs or to help colour out and disguise marks. Some stains can be bought in liquid form, but for the best range of tones and colours you will need to buy stains in powder form, ready to be mixed with spirit or water.

Spirit-based stains, usually mixed with methylated spirits (methyl alcohol), are quick-drying, because the spirit rapidly evaporates in air. This makes them unsuitable for use on large areas, as some areas will dry before others, causing an uneven finish. Spirit stains are usually applied after polishing. If the polish is applied on top of the stain, the spirit in the polish will dilute the stain and lighten the surface colour.

Water-based stains dry more slowly, making them suitable for large areas because they give an even finish. They are generally applied before polishing. One disadvantage, however, is that they can raise the grain, which will then need to be flattened before you can proceed any further. Both spirit and water stains can be thinned after application by adding further spirit/water.

Left: *Stains often have to be tailor-made to suit the job in hand.*

Below: *Stains can be purchased in colour powder form, which are then mixed with a suitable solvent.*

Other stains, such as coloured waxes, are not frequently used in furniture restoration. Their use is generally confined to moderating the colour of a surface slightly after it has been polished.

Stains can be applied by brush, which should be thoroughly cleaned after use with a cloth or by a dowel with some cloth wrapped around the end, known as a swab (see p.52). Alternatively, some polish can be mixed with a small amount of stain and applied not with a rubber but with a fad. This allows the whole area to be slightly tinted, and it overcomes the problem of the spirit base making the colour lighter.

Mixing a spirit-based stain

1 Aways use a clean container and a flat-bladed knife or small teaspoon for mixing stains. Methylated spirits (methyl alcohol) is an ideal spirit liquid mixer.

2 Pour the required quantity of methylated spirits into the clean container. It is better to add powder to liquid rather than liquid to powder, in order to avoid unnecessary wastage. Select the correct powder required for the colour effect desired, and add a small amount at a time.

3 Mix with a clean brush. If a stronger stain tone is needed, simply add further powder. When you have finished with the stain, pour away the unused stain and clean all the utensils and the brush to ensure that the next coloured stain to be mixed is not tinted with any residue from this one.

LEATHER

One of the most commonly used writing surfaces for a desk or writing table of the 17th, 18th or 19th century was leather. The leather was often decorated with bandings applied with a hot tooling wheel. The original patinated leather, if surviving, will add great character and warmth to any piece. However, often due to its very nature, over time the leather will dry out and perish, leading to the need for a replacement to be fitted.

Since the 17th century, leather has been used as a covering on desk tops and also inset into writing surfaces. Nineteenth-century leather tops are not unusual on antique furniture, and occasionally, if it has been treated carefully, you may even find a desk or table with the original leather from the 18th century. In the majority of cases, however, cracking, tearing or wear will mean that the leather surface has to be replaced.

There are basically two types of leather to choose from: skiver (sheep leather) and hide (cow leather). Skiver is found in smaller pieces and often used on davenport tops, bureau falls (the interior of a bureau, which is used as a writing surface) and writing boxes. For larger desks and writing table tops, hide is the obvious choice due to its generally larger size. Also, as a rule of thumb, hide tends to be of better quality and more suited to quality antique furniture than skiver.

When selecting the hide or skiver for use, try to find a piece that has little or no scarring on the surface and avoid leather taken from the neck area, which tends to have stretch marks. The leather will be applied to the desk or table in its natural tan colour and will be coloured when it is in situ. Also, it is vital that the surface on to which the leather is going to be laid is level, with no cracks or splits, because these will become visible through the leather.

With the leather laid and coloured, the decorative bandings, known as tooling, must be decided upon. There are two basic types: gold tooling and blind tooling. Both are applied using a hot tooling wheel (see p.75), which embosses a pattern on to the leather surface.

The difference between the two types of tooling is that the gold tooling is applied after the top has been laid and coloured, while blind tooling is embossed into the top when the leather is still wet and uncoloured, and the deep imprint is then coloured with a suitable stain.

The gold tooling effect is obtained with the tooling wheel running over a gold foil ribbon, which leaves a gold pattern. The type and style of decorative

Above: *Tooling wheels are used when heated to spitting heat. Firm and even pressure produces an excellent result.*

pattern used will often reflect the period of the piece of furniture, and a wide range of styles are available.

Above: *In "blind tooling", the tooling wheel is used without the roll of gold leaf.*

Right: *A selection of patterned borders that are available on decorative tooling wheels.*

HANDLES AND HINGES

Handles have changed greatly during the centuries in style, decoration and the materials used to make them. They were often replaced not because the originals had worn but to keep pace with the ever-changing fashions of the period. Sometimes the replacements were out of keeping with the style of the piece. Hinges were less influenced by fashion, although some were made to be more decorative to complement other furniture hardware.

THE EARLY BEGINNINGS

During medieval times, the earliest hollowed-out coffers may have had wooden peg hinges, but it was not long before the metal strap hinge began to be used. With the arrival of the plank coffer, the use of metal greatly increased. Indeed, the box chests or coffers of the 14th and 15th centuries would often have been bound with iron bands to make them stronger and to protect against splitting. By the beginning of the 15th century, hinges were becoming more elaborate with butterfly hinges, so called because they resembled butterfly wings, being used, often embossed with punched and engraved decoration.

Handles of the period tended to be ring-like in form and, like the hinges, manufactured in iron.

Left: *This 15th-century oak coffer features the stout, metal strap hinges which are typical of the period.*

THE 17TH CENTURY

The major changes began during the mid- to latter part of the 17th century. By this period, the business of manufacturing hinges, handles and locks (see pp.40–41) was becoming more of a specialized field. Iron was rapidly being replaced by an alloy of copper and zinc that formed the more malleable brass. Equally, the local smith was being replaced by more specialized craftsmen, from the designer and carver of the model handle, to the moulder who cast the handle and finally to the man who would chaste (carve) any pattern or design into the surface. The handle would then have the edges chamfered and be polished with a coat of lacquering to stop any tarnishing. By the mid-18th century, fire gilding (see p.39) was used on the finest of pieces.

THE 18TH CENTURY

Until the early 18th century, brass handles had been secured to the drawer with thin iron strips, or straps as they were known. From that time on, they were replaced with cast posts, or pummels, which were attached with threaded nuts to the back of the drawer.

During the late 17th century and early part of the 18th century, plate and open plate handles, which could be plain or engraved, would be made *en suite* with

Right: *This 18th-century open plate handle and matching escutcheon are typical of their period.*

Above: *Hinges could be decorative, as well as functional, but each was designed for a specific purpose.*

Left: For the keen restorer, it is a good idea to collect antique handles and store for future renovation projects.

matching escutcheons to give a more consistent and balanced appearance to a piece of furniture.

During the early 18th century, the hardware would in all likelihood have been made by a local foundry. From the mid part of the century the trade became more centralized. The new foundries made handles in many different styles for the home market, but handles and other brassware were also exported, most notably for use on American and Dutch furniture.

Another material used occasionally during this period was paktong. It was an alloy of copper and zinc with nickel added to make it look like silver in appearance but at a fraction of the cost. Originally imported from the Orient, where it had been used for some time previously, it was often found on export furniture or as decorative mounts on knifeboxes.

By the latter part of the 18th century, the fashion had moved once again toward plate handles. Differing from the earlier 18th-century examples, which were cast, they were often stamped out of sheet brass, which would have had a higher copper content, making the metal more malleable. Often decorative, their centres would carry designs that, like the knob handles that followed them during the early part of the 19th century, reflected the fashion and themes of the time, with the lion mask and the Prince of Wales feather plumes both featuring heavily.

THE 19TH CENTURY

By this time, the number of foundries had greatly increased and the range of published designs had also multiplied. It is interesting to note, however, that during this period the fashion for wooden knob handles took hold. Frequently, the original brassware was removed from 18th-century furniture to be replaced with large and, most would agree, unsightly wooden examples.

Above: *18th-century swan-neck handles in various styles ranging from plain to rococco.*

Right: *A selection of 18th- and 19th-century cast knobs and pressed plate handles.*

Left: *An 18th-century card table hinge, which is distinctive because it allows the top to open then sit level with the opposite side.*

Right: *When removing antique metal care should be taken as they may be brittle and can be easily damaged.*

REPLACING HANDLES

During the centuries fashion and tastes have constantly changed, and owners often replaced perfectly serviceable hardware with something more "fashionable". So, in terms of restoration, handles are frequently replaced to bring a piece back to its original state rather than to correct any damage. To select the right kind of replacement, you will need to consult reference books and study the various styles of brassware. You might also find clues by looking for marks and shadows on the furniture, which might indicate the size and type of fitting used when the piece was first made.

Frequently, replacement handles will not have been attached to drawer and door fronts in the same way. Using the Victorian wooden door knobs as an example again, these were often attached with large screws. These holes can be disguised in a variety of ways, either by selecting plate handles which cover the damage, or by patching the holes.

Occasionally, an original handle, one of a pair or a set, may be missing. There are three main options open to you in this case: you could try and find a match from another piece of furniture or from a breaker collection; order a single replacement or a whole new set from a manufacturer specializing in period handles; or commission a copy to be made by a specialist foundry, which will use the same techniques today as were used in centuries past. Copy casting involves one of two methods: sand casting and the lost-wax process, which are explained here (see box, right).

Making copies

When the profile of the item of metalware is not too elaborate, the sand-casting process will be used. This involves placing the template piece into a two-part mould, each part of which is packed with fine casting sand. The box is then carefully separated and the template removed, leaving its profile in the sand. The two halves of the mould are then rejoined and molten brass poured in. When cool, the box is opened to reveal the newly cast metalware.

The sand-casting method, while ideal for plain metalware, is unsuitable for a more elaborate design that may have undercuts or intricate patterns. These would be lost when the piece was lifted from the sand prior to casting, and so in these cases the lost-wax technique would be used.

In the example illustrated below, one of a pair of escutcheons is missing and a copy needs to be made. Because the design of the escutcheon is very intricate and detailed, the sand-casting technique would not be suitable, whereas the lost-wax process is ideal.

First, a rubber mould is made of the escutcheon. The mould is made in two parts, each with locating pins, which allows the remaining escutcheon, which is being used as a template, to be easily removed. The empty mould is then rejointed and liquid wax poured into it. This will create a perfect replica of the escutcheon, capturing all the detail of the carving.

When the mould is cool and the wax has hardened, the wax copy is removed from the rubber mould. It is then encased in a two-part plaster mould and heated, which both hardens the plaster and melts the wax, creating a perfect hollow profile of the original escutcheon. Molten brass is then poured into the plaster mould, forcing out the liquid wax.

Left: *When the mould has cooled again, it is opened to reveal an excellent copy of the original escutcheon. Once cleaned, it can be coloured and lacquered to match the original.*

MOUNTS, CASTORS AND METALWARE

The range of mounts, castors and other metalware is vast and is influenced by the date, style and country of origin. In the past, such items were ordered from the local foundry when needed. Indeed, at times a strong indication of the piece's original maker can be gained simply by studying its original metalware. By the 18th century, the foundries were beginning to publish designs and you can often find their name stamped into a hinge, castor or lock.

Unlike today, when screws, nails and brass fittings are factory-made in their tens of thousands, the brassware and fixings of the previous centuries were all hand-made. Clout nails, which had roughly shaped heads, and hand-made screws, which had off-centre, hand-cut slots, were all works of art in their own right. It is a testament to their quality that, some 300 years after being made, they can be fixed back into their original locations ready to be used again.

As with the breaker store for wood (see p.26), or the veneer store for old surface veneers (see p.28), an equally important part of any restoration workshop is the brasswork store. Any old nails, screws or brassware that are removed from a piece of furniture are kept here for future use. While skilled foundries can make copies of period mounts, castors and galleries (small ornamental railings surrounding the top of a desk, table, etc.), there is still no substitute for the original. Each piece of bespoke brassware was designed for its particular role.

Above: *A selection of metalware dating from the 18th and 19th centuries, including mounts, castors and a section of gallery.*

Left: *A mid-18th-century Louis XV Japanese lacquer commode is richly embellished with ormolu mounts.*

Above: *A selection of 18th- and 19th-century brass castors, which, in spite of years of use, are still in working order.*

During the 18th and 19th centuries, there were two methods of treating brassware once it had been cast to prevent tarnishing: fire gilding and lacquering. Fire gilding was an expensive process usually reserved for the finest mounts, galleries and handles. The process involved mixing mercury with gold, applying it to the metalware and then heating it. The mercury would evaporate and the gold would bind to the metal. This gave a rich, bold finish, but, due to the mercury fumes that were constantly being given off, the life of the mercury gilder was a short one. The second method, lacquering, gave a similiar, if not quite as rich, appearance to fire gilding. Unfortunately, the use of abrasive solvents for cleaning over the years means that the majority of handles have lost their original finishes, but when fire-gilt and lacquered finishes are still largely intact, they should be cleaned with care. For the most part, such finishes require little more than an occasional wipe with a damp cloth.

Blunting a nail

1 *Knocking a large nail into a hard piece of wood, such as oak, can cause splitting. This is due to the fact that the sharp point is acting as a wedge.*

2 *An easy step to counter this is to blunt the point of the nail prior to use.*

3 *Just one or two taps with the hammer are needed to gain the desired effect.*

4 *With the tip now blunted, you can hammer the nail through the wood without it splitting.*

Removing a nail

1 *When a nail needs to be removed from a polished surface, the pliers should not touch the wood as illustrated here.*

2 *The pressure caused by the pliers bearing down on the wood can often cause bruising and marking to the surface polish.*

3 *The preferred method is to place another layer between the pliers and the polished surface. In this instance, a cabinet scraper is being used. Equally acceptable is a thin piece of wood, etc.*

LOCKS AND KEYS

The range of types of key is vast, and all workshops should keep as many as possible. Often the more simple lock can be operated with a replacement key that may require little or no alteration. These antique keys can be sourced in many locations ranging from junk shops to local bric-à-brac markets. Replacement blanks, which can be cut to fit locks, are also available and can be sourced from suitable specialist suppliers.

The earliest known locks date from the Egyptian times, around 2000 BC, and the Romans also manufactured and used them. Their use continued through the ages, and by the 14th century locks were not uncommon on English furniture. Indeed, examples from the 14th and 15th centuries are to be found, with their distinctive feature of a flush face plate and sunken movement, both making sure that they could not be prised open. By the latter part of the 15th century, locks were becoming more decorative and their use increasingly widespread. In these periods, it was not only gold and valuables that required safe keeping but equally so correspondence, as a letter swearing allegiance to the wrong party could result in an untimely end.

By the late 17th century, elaborate locks were still in use, but the increasing manufacture of chests and other cabinet furniture meant that a plainer steel lock was being used, often with a simple throw mechanism. As furniture designs became more elaborate, so the need for a more tailored lock increased. Bureaux required angled face plates to mirror the fall, cupboard locks could be designed to throw either left or right and, where extra security was required, such as with an escritoire, three- or four-pin locks were used, which made their forcing open very difficult. On continental locks, one often finds a double throw movement, which increases the length the bolt is extended into the lock housing, thereby helping to strengthen the security of the lock.

During the 18th century, brass began to be used on the better-quality locks, although cheaper locks were still made from iron. Their manufacture began to be more elaborate, and, in 1778, a major watershed was reached when Robert Barron designed a revolutionary lever system that, unlike previous locks, which had operated on a ward system and relied on a single tumbler, operated with two tumblers, meaning that in order for the lock to throw open, the tumblers had to be lifted both back and up to a precise height. This lever system still exists in today's locks.

The lock was further developed during the 18th century by Bramah, who, in 1784, patented a system that incorporated a tube-like key with notches on the end that fitted into a lock fitted with springs, meaning that the key had to fit precisely into position in order for the lock to work. Even a slight variation would mean that the lock did not throw, and therefore a very specific key had to be used with each lock. If the key was lost, cutting a new one was a specialist task that required a trained locksmith.

It is rare that a maker would use only one specific lock or key in his furniture making, although one such exception is that of the 18th-century designer and

Left: *It is important to carry a wide selection of locks and keys salvaged from breaker chests and cabinets.*

Right: *A selection of Bramah locks with their distinctive patent pattern mark.*

furniture-maker Thomas Chippendale. The use of the S key and corresponding escutcheon, while not proved to be exclusive, is widely accepted by academics and collectors alike as a mark of a piece made by Chippendale. Documented examples are to be found on pieces at Brocket Hall, Harewood House and Nostell Priory, all of which are Chippendale commissions.

While general servicing and key replacement should be able to be carried out by a competent restoration workshop, it should be remembered that some locks are very elaborate, and these more complicated examples are better dealt with by a specialist locksmith or restorer.

Above: *During the 18th and 19th centuries, a variety of locks were developed each with a specific role or task to perform.*

Servicing a lock

1 *Over the years working locks can collect all kinds of debris, such as dust, wax and even insect remains, that will eventually make the lock less efficient. A quick service is all that is needed.*

2 *Remove the lock and place it flat on a clean surface. Unscrew the retaining screws from the back plate. Take care not to misplace the original screws.*

3 *Slide the screwdriver carefully between the face and back plate and gently ease it off making sure not to damage either piece. You will now be able to see if there is any debris collected in the lock's workings.*

4 *Gently remove any debris with a soft brush. Check for any other damage while the back plate is off. If there is any rusting or parts have broken away, restoration must be carried out by a specialist locksmith.*

5 *When the lock is clean, lubricate the internal workings using a dry silicon lubricant spray. Do not use oil-based lubricants as they will quickly attract dust and cause the same problem over time.*

6 *Check that the lock works freely, then replace the back plate using the original screws. Check the lock again before placing the lock back in its original position.*

Restoration techniques

Cabinets and especially chests of drawers, by the very nature of their design, will have a number of restoration requirements that are unique to them alone. Working parts such as drawers may need their runners or stops replaced. Drawer linings will shrink, causing splits. Doors may need reglazing or refitting and, on rare occasions, the entire carcass may need to be dismantled and reglued.

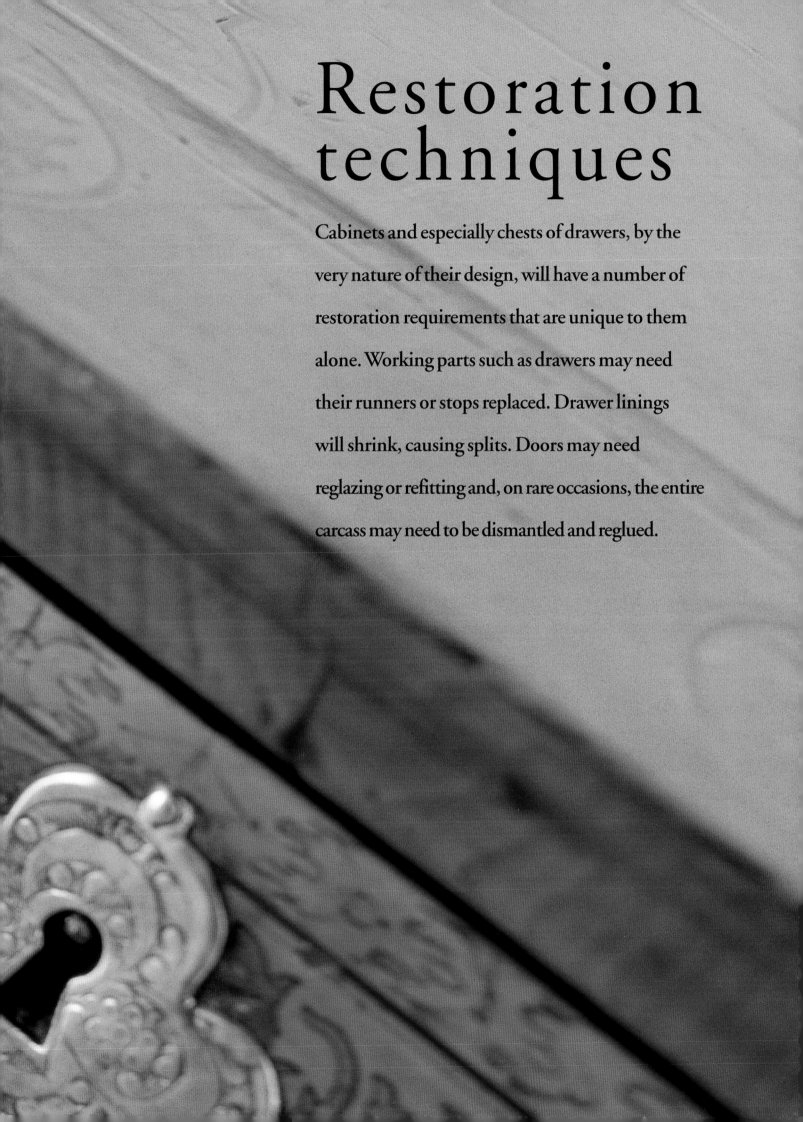

DISMANTLING AND REBUILDING CHESTS

It is unusual to have to dismantle a chest of drawers, but you may have to do this when a chest has become very loose or when a side or top has been badly damaged and must be removed from the chest in order to be repaired.

The techniques required and steps taken are equally applicable for the majority of carcass furniture, such as bureaus, bookcases or tallboys. The main consideration is to examine the construction of the piece closely prior to commencement to make sure that no unnecessary damage is caused to either the constituent parts or joints during the dismantling process. All polished areas should be laid on a protective surface and any hammer blows or pressure to dismantle joints should be applied next to joints to ensure that no unnecessary splintering occurs.

Dismantling the chest

This George III chest, c.1760, has become loose and a split has appeared in the top. It is a typical example of 18th-century carcass construction, and closer examination shows that there are no through dovetails that have been veneered over, and no nails or screws have been added to give strength at a later date. Before any work can be done, the chest must be dismantled.

MATERIALS AND EQUIPMENT
- chalk
- hardwood lengths and blocks
- nails
- hammers
- mallet
- wide chisel
- flat-bladed knife

1 The back of the chest consists of a number of boards. Their location should be marked before removal; a suitable method is to mark them with chalk lines, as shown here.

2 Remove the backboards by placing a length of hardwood against the location of the holding nails and tapping it with a hammer. Make sure that only the areas nailed are struck, to avoid unnecessary splintering of the boards.

3 Remove the kickers, which help to make the drawers run level, as well as the wedges, which hold the dust boards in place, by using a mallet to tap a wide chisel between each board and kicker.

◁ 4 Remove both facing strips, which cover the rebates (rabbets) for the dust boards along the front edges, by sliding a flat-bladed knife along the glue line. Use a hammer to help the knife move down each facing edge.

5 Remove the dust boards from the long drawers by knocking them out either backward or forward (depending on the construction of the chest). Place a hardwood block between the board and hammer to avoid any unnecessary damage to the wood.

6 As well as being nailed together, the top and side joints are given extra strength by glue blocks. Remove these by placing a chisel behind each block in turn and giving it a sharp blow with a mallet. The glue line holding the blocks should come away easily.

7 Having removed the dust boards from the long drawers, there still remains the frame from the two short drawers, which is jointed with the twin drawer centre stile. In this case the joint is a through tenon, and therefore the stile and frame must be knocked apart.

◁ 8 Remove the top from the sides using a hammer and hardwood block as for the backboards. Slide out the remaining dust board. Now lift the remainder of the carcass clear of the workbench with the aid of a helper and place it the right way up.

▷

Dismantling the chest...continued

◁ **9** Now dismantle the sides, which are dovetailed into the base, using a hammer and hardwood block, as before. Tap the base while lifting one side clear, then repeat for the other side.

▽ **10** The chest is now dismantled. The feet have not been removed, to prevent further damage to the chest of

Reassembling the chest

When the necessary repairs have been made (in this case, the table had developed a split top, which needed gluing together), the chest of drawers can be rebuilt.

MATERIALS AND EQUIPMENT
- toothbrush
- PVA (white) glue
- cloths (rags)
- sash clamps
- clamping blocks
- snap clamps
- gauge sticks
- hammer
- length of hardwood
- masking tape
- nails
- animal glue
- rubber
- polish
- wax

1 Remove traces of the old animal glue using an old toothbrush and hot water. The water will soften the glue and enable it to be removed without any damage to the actual joints.

◁ **2** Apply only a small amount of PVA (white) glue to the joints between the sides and bottom, then refit the sides and the drawer frame. Wipe away any excess glue with a cloth (cotton rag) immediately. Apply sash clamps and a snap clamp.

3 Before the glue sets, fit a drawer to check that the drawer frame is square, and check the carcass for squareness using gauge sticks.

◁ **5** Glue the top back on and clamp it securely into place with snap clamps and sash clamps. Refit the old glue blocks using animal glue. Leave to dry. Also reglue the facing strips, holding them in position with masking tape while they dry.

4 Slide the long dust boards back into position, then gently tap the kickers and wedges back into place using a length of hardwood to guard against unnecessary bruising.

◁ **6** Finally, nail the backboards back into place, remembering to match up the chalk lines to ensure the correct positioning.

Right: *With the chest reassembled, any surfaces that need it can be revived, polished and waxed, and any missing handles replaced.*

POLISHING AND COLOURING

The term "polishing" is used to describe the overall method of filling the grain and enhancing the figure of any piece of wood using shellac polish. The vast majority of polishing work today is commonly known as French polishing, which involves the use of shellac polish combined with oil – often linseed oil – and applied to the wood with a linen rubber.

Within the history of antique furniture, however, there are two very distinctive methods of finishing: varnishing using oil or spirit varnishes, and French polishing, which was introduced only in the 19th century. Both methods create distinctive appearances, and it is the effects of light, oxidation and time that make these polished and waxed surfaces so sought after by today's collectors.

The principles involved in polishing a new surface or repolishing an old surface remain the same: numerous thin layers are built up to form a combined surface. When completed, the polish should have a translucent quality that allows the colour and figure of the wood beneath to be seen. On occasion it may be necessary to tint the polish in order to adjust the final colour. This method of colouring is different from staining with spirit, water or oil, which is the process by which the actual wood tone is changed rather than simply colouring or tinting the polish.

When removing polish from a piece of furniture, it must be done a layer at a time to minimize any damage to the colour and surface of the piece. When the damaged areas have been carefully lifted, further polish can again be applied, a layer at a time, until the required surface appearance is obtained. If too much polish is applied the surface will have a treacle-like appearance; if too little polish is used the grain in the wood will look open and "hungry", resulting in a blotchy effect once the surface has been waxed.

French polishing

Prior to the early 19th century the methods of finishing furniture were mainly the application of varnishes or oils such as linseed and various wax compounds. These were usually applied, often by brush or cloth (cotton rag), after the grain had been sealed with ground brick dust or pumice powder. They served to protect the wood and could be burnished to a soft lustre finish.

In 1820 a new practice, imported from France, came to favour. It was the use of shellac, which comes from the shells of the lac beetle. The shellac, which was dissolved in spirit, was applied layer by layer, giving a hard, glossy finish. Over the years, and with the application of wax, the hard, glossy surfaces mellow, and depending on the style and period of the piece, the surface finish can range from hard and glossy to a soft, almost matt appearance.

MATERIALS AND EQUIPMENT

- wadding (batting)
- linen
- polish
- fine wire (steel) wool
- methylated spirits (methyl alcohol)
- soft cloth (cotton rag)
- shellac
- linseed oil
- clear beeswax

Left: *This Regency table has become severely damaged on its polished surface and must be repolished.*

MAKING AND CHARGING A RUBBER

A rubber is an essential tool for applying a French polish finish and is easy to make. All you need is some wadding (batting) or plain unmedicated cotton wool and a square of linen or similar lint-free cloth. The rubber acts in the same manner as a sponge, absorbing a quantity of the polish (known as charging), which is squeezed out on to the surface being polished when you apply pressure to it. A rubber can also be used to apply a stain to wood.

▷ **1** Lay a 15cm/6in long piece of wadding (batting) on the centre of a piece of linen the size of a large handkerchief.

2 Fold the ends of the linen inward and grasp them in the centre of your palm.

3 With all the outer edges gathered together, twist the ends of the linen to form a tail.

4 The rubber is complete when the tail is completely twisted. For a smaller, more intricate, polishing job, make a smaller rubber to suit.

◁ **5** To charge the rubber, open out the linen to expose the wadding, then pour a small amount of polish on to the wadding. With practice, you will be able to judge the correct quantity. Note that if the rubber is too dry it will not run smoothly over the surface; if it is too wet it will simply lay the polish on the surface.

▷ **6** Refold the linen around the wadding. Squeeze the tail to apply pressure to the wadding, to force the polish through the linen. The more you tighten the tail, the more polish will emerge. After polishing, you can store the rubber for another day.

▷

APPLYING THE POLISH

If the damage to a surface is extensive, it will have to be stripped back with methylated spirits (methyl alcohol) before repolishing, as shown here. New wood is polished in much the same way, except that the grain is first filled with pumice and polish, then sanded flat with very fine or broken down sandpaper.

Once the rubber has been charged, the polish can be applied. This process takes time, and the finish must be left overnight for the polish to harden before it can be buffed to a high sheen or cut back to produce a matt finish.

Tip

When polishing with a rubber (step 3) the idea is to "body up" or fill the grain. This is done by first applying the polish in straight continuous strokes along the grain (below top). The polish is then applied in circular motions (below centre) and finally with wider figure of eight movements (below bottom).

1 Remove the old polish and wax surface with fine wire (steel) wool and methylated spirits (methyl alcohol).

2 Once the old polish and wax have been removed, wash off the surface with a soft cloth (cotton rag) and methylated spirits.

3 Polish the surface using a rubber and shellac (see Tip). Linseed oil can be dripped on to the surface to help lubricate the rubber. This technique, known as "bodying up", fills the grain. Leave for at least 24 hours to harden.

4 When the polish has hardened, cut it back lightly using fine wire wool and working in the direction of the grain. Use light strokes to remove any raised nibs of polish. This also produces a higher gloss finish.

5 Finally, apply a coat of wax. Use light strokes as the polished surface will still be delicate. Allow to stand for a week before use to allow the polish to fully harden.

Right: *When polished, the scratches become invisible and the table has an even, soft sheen that should last for years.*

Waxing

All antique furniture will require waxing during its lifetime. Waxing feeds, protects and nourishes the wood. It is the combination of waxes with natural grease and oxidation that forms the surface patination that is so desirable. Over the generations, various types of wax have been used, with workshops producing their own secret recipes.

One of the most common misconceptions is that the more frequently a piece is waxed. the fuller the finish will be. Over-waxing will result in smeary surfaces, since wax softens wax.

The only remedy for this is to remove all the wax and begin afresh. It is far better to wax at sensible intervals and apply only a very thin layer. Use only natural wax-based products.

WAXING A FLAT SURFACE

1 Apply a thin layer of wax using a soft cloth (cotton rag) impregnated with the chosen wax. Never apply too thick a layer, as this will simply make the rubbing up more difficult and time consuming.

2 Even out the wax using a soft brush. Take care not to mark the surface and make sure you work along the direction of the grain. Use long, steady strokes, working from one side of the surface to the other.

3 Allow the wax to harden for a few minutes, then buff the surface vigorously with a soft cloth, working in the direction of the grain. Finally, use a clean cloth to give the surface a final burnish.

WAXING A CARVED SURFACE

  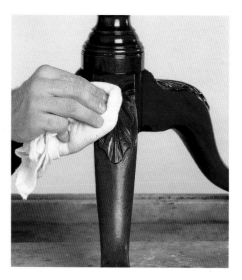

1 Due to the nature of the hollows and relief, it is better to apply a thin coat of wax with a soft brush, making sure that it is neither too hard nor too soft.

2 Allow the wax to harden for a few minutes, then gently burnish the carving with a soft brush. This will remove any surplus wax and even out what remains.

3 Finally, buff the highlights using a soft cloth (cotton rag). Mutton cloth, which is available from most trade suppliers, is ideal for this role.

Staining

Paints and varnishes adhere to the surface of the wood, but stains penetrate it, changing its colour permanently. For this reason, stains are favoured by the restorer. They can enrich dull-looking wood or change the colour of new wood so that it blends in with the rest of the piece of furniture. This bureau has had a new piece of wood added to it that must be stained and polished so that it matches the rest of the piece.

MATERIALS AND EQUIPMENT

- spirit-based (alcohol-based) stain
- cloth (cotton rag)
- wooden dowel
- fine brush
- rubbers
- polish
- methylated spirits (methyl alcohol)
- soft brush
- wax

Tip

Spirit-based (alcohol-based) stains, thinned with methylated spirits (methyl alcohol), are the best stains to use, because they dry very quickly. However, they are harder to obtain and more difficult to use. This is because they can leave obvious overlap marks. Solvent- and water-based stains are available ready mixed and are easier to apply.

1 Use a spirit-based (alcohol-based) stain mixed to match the colour of the furniture. For a small area like this, wrap a piece of cloth (cotton rag) around one end of a dowel and use this to apply the stain to the new piece of wood. If staining a large area, use a brush to apply the stain. Continue until the colour is even, then leave to dry.

2 Check again that the stain is even. If necessary, add another layer, or draw in the grain with a fine brush (see p.53). When you are satisfied with the colour of the dried stain, charge a rubber with polish and apply a layer to the stain, and also to the rest of the bureau to blend in the stained area (see pp.49–50). Allow the polish to dry.

3 Cut back the polish with a rubber charged with a little methylated spirits (methyl alcohol). The new wood should now be indistinguishable from the old.

4 Use a soft brush to apply a thin coat of wax to the new wood, and the rest of the piece of furniture, to give a soft, even sheen. Leave to dry.

Above: *Now stained and polished, the new wood blends seamlessly with the old.*

Graining

During the late 18th and early 19th centuries, rosewood was imported from India, South America and the West Indies for use in the manufacture of furniture. It was an expensive wood, and so only the finest pieces of furniture were made from solid rosewood; other pieces were made from beech, which was a hard-grained, easily workable, cheap native wood. The beech was "grained" with a paint finish to give the appearance of rosewood. Over time, the areas of graining wear away, revealing the beech underneath, as has happened with this Regency chair. In this case, it is necessary to simulate the rosewood graining while also giving it a patinated, antique look. The techniques for distressing are varied and include using smooth stones, fine wire (steel) wool and homemade tools. These should be practised and perfected before use.

MATERIALS AND EQUIPMENT
- light brown spirit-based (alcohol-based) stain
- fine brushes
- screwdriver
- rubber
- polish
- dark brown spirit-based stain
- wax
- cloth (cotton rag)

Above: *An area of the graining has worn away on the chair leg to reveal the beech wood underneath.*

1 Apply a base coat of a light brown stain mixed to match the base colour of the rest of the chair (see p.52). Leave to dry. Charge a rubber with polish and apply a thin layer.

2 Apply a dark brown stain mixed to match the grain of the simulated rosewood, using a fine brush to replicate the pattern. If no residue of graining is left, use a piece of patinated rosewood veneer as a pattern.

3 When the graining is dry, distress the graining effect using a screwdriver, if necessary, to match the original. Give it another rubber of polish to seal in the effect, then wax the chair using a cloth.

Above: *The grained beech chair, on the right of the picture, now looks very similar to the solid rosewood chair on the left. Both these chairs are dining chairs, made c.1810.*

REPAIRING CARCASSES AND TOPS

Traditionally, carcasses are very strong and rarely suffer serious structural damage in normal use. Exceptions occur when changes in humidity cause carcasses and tops to crack, heavy doors put undue strain on hinges, and plinths and feet become scuffed and damaged. None of these problems is insurmountable, provided the correct repair and restoration techniques are employed, and the results can be very pleasing.

Repairing a split top

Changes in humidity can cause chest tops to split in exactly the same way that table tops split. If a split occurs along the line where two pieces of wood are joined, they can simply be reglued and clamped to secure. If a split occurs away from a natural join, the top must be repaired with butterfly keys.

This c.1845 pine chest of drawers, veneered in Cuban mahogany, has a split top, due to the pine core shrinking away from the mahogany until the resulting tension caused the core to split apart. The mouldings must be removed, the split must be separated and reglued and then re-secured with butterfly keys, glued into cut-outs routed into the underside of the top.

Above: *The split in the top.*

MATERIALS AND EQUIPMENT

- hammer
- hardwood block
- flat-bladed knife
- tenon saw
- PVA (white) glue
- sash clamps
- clamping blocks
- softwood
- deep-throated clamps
- cardboard
- utility knife
- router
- chisel
- jack plane
- water-based stain
- fine brushes
- cabinet scraper
- fine-grade sandpaper
- rubber
- polish
- stopping wax
- spirit-based (alcohol-based) stain
- cloth (cotton rag)
- wax

1 Remove the top from the carcass using a hammer and hardwood block and place it upside down on a protected workbench. Blocks of wood had been glued to the underside in a previous attempt to repair the split. Remove these now with a flat-bladed knife, then turn the top over.

2 Carefully cut the mahogany long-grain mouldings that pass the end of the split from the pine core with a tenon saw. The mouldings have not split, and so they can be removed intact and reglued later (see step 5). Apply PVA (white) glue along the split in the top.

3 Clamp the width of the top together using sash clamps and clamping blocks. Place a piece of paper, then a piece of softwood, along the length of the split, then secure both with deep-throated clamps to make sure the two parts of the top remain level. Leave to dry.

4 Cut butterfly keys from pine and rout matching holes along the underside of the split (see p.72). Glue in the keys and plane them down until flush with the underside. Stain the keys to match the top.

5 Turn the top over and work along the split with a cabinet scraper to remove any loose veneer. Take great care to scrape only along the split, to avoid damaging the rest of the veneer. Reglue any un-split mouldings.

6 Smooth the area along the split by rubbing with fine-grade sandpaper. Avoid sanding too wide an area around the split.

7 Charge a rubber with polish and apply a layer to the split area to conceal any tiny missing areas of veneer (see pp.49–50). The split will now be almost invisible.

8 Select a stopping wax to match the colour and tone of the veneer. Fill the small areas of missing veneer with the wax, using a flat-bladed knife.

9 Mix a spirit-based (alcohol-based) stain to match the colour and tone of the veneer (see p.33), and apply it to the sanded and polished area. This will blend the two pieces together and help to mask the joint.

10 Put the top back on. Treat the entire top with a wax chosen to match the colour and tone of the veneer. Take care not to rub too hard on the split area, because you risk removing the applied colour and wax.

Left: *Now stained and waxed, the split is almost invisible. With the inset butterfly keys on the underside securing the joint, no further restoration should be necessary.*

Replacing a bracket foot

The bracket foot was introduced during the early 18th century and remained basically unchanged in its construction through the rest of the century. When replacing a single missing foot, you can copy one of the remaining feet, but if all the feet are missing you will need to seek advice from an expert in this field to determine the correct shape and style required. This chest of drawers is missing one of its mahogany feet, although some of the glue blocks remain.

MATERIALS AND EQUIPMENT
- cardboard
- utility knife
- mahogany
- coping saw or band saw
- jack plane
- mitre box
- scotch glue
- spring clips
- softwood
- rasp
- chisel
- screwdriver
- rubber
- polish
- fine brush
- stain

1 Make a cardboard template (pattern) of one of the remaining feet and mark this outline twice on the selected old surface mahogany, once for each side of the foot.

2 Cut out both pieces of the foot by hand with a coping saw or by machine with a band saw. Plane the joining mitres with a jack plane, ideally using a mitre box.

3 Attach both parts of the foot to the carcass and each other with scotch glue. Rub each part back and forth a few times to create suction between the foot and carcass, then apply pressure with spring clips.

◁ **4** Cut new glue blocks from softwood. With the clips still in place, glue these blocks, into position and secure them with more spring clips. Leave them slightly proud of the foot so that they can be trimmed flush later. This will help to distribute the weight of the chest.

5 If the foot parts were cut with a band saw, use a rasp to remove the blade marks that will have been left. Note the wear patterns on the opposite original foot and try to mirror them.

6 Trim the glue blocks flush with a chisel or plane. Round over all the sharp edges with the shank of a screwdriver. This mimics the natural process of years of waxing and handling. Also, if a clean piece of mahogany has been used to make the foot, add a few knocks to match the existing feet.

Left: Polish the exterior of the foot, and stain the interior and the glue blocks. The new foot now matches the carcass in grain, colour and finish. The wear and patination also match the other feet on the chest, and no casual observer should be able to spot the replacement.

Spring clips

There are numerous types of clamp designed to help in the restoration of antique furniture. One of the most versatile, used for difficult and awkward clamping, is the spring clip. This is home-made from old upholstery springs, and is ideal for applying pressure or simply holding small pieces of wood or furniture in place.

◁ *1 Choose a large old upholstery spring; this will allow you to make several clips of different sizes. The spring steel will keep its shape and will apply considerable pressure when pulled apart.*

2 Using a bench grinder, cut through the tensile-steel spring at two points to form a circular clip, the two ends of which should meet. When pulled apart, the natural curve of the spring should give the necessary pressure to hold any parts together.

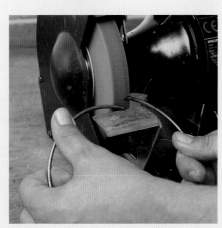

3 Grind a point on each end of the clip. These points will make sure that the clip remains in place when it is being used.

4 When completed, the clip can be used for a variety of awkward clamping tasks. To keep the tension, push the two end points until they overlap, then pull them apart and place them in the required holding position.

REPAIRING DRAWERS

Prior to the late 17th century, the majority of drawers would have run on rebated (rabbeted) side drawer runners. After this time, the runners were fitted on the bottom of the drawer. Due to their constant action, drawer stops and drawer runners are sometimes worn away. A sure sign that they need to be replaced is when a drawer begins to stick. Failure to attend to this can, in extreme cases, make the chest unusable.

Replacing cock beading

Cock beading is the name given to the moulding that runs around the edge of inset drawers. This decorative feature, which was introduced during the early 18th century, also protects the edge of applied veneers from flaking and splitting. Sometimes the beading can become loose or broken due to being snagged. On this drawer, part of the beading had become detached and lost and another part was damaged.

MATERIALS AND EQUIPMENT
- paring chisel
- mahogany
- utility knife
- PVA (white) glue
- spring clips
- block plane
- fine-grade sandpaper
- fine brush
- stain
- rubber
- polish

1 Using a paring chisel, remove the damaged area of cock beading. Select a piece of mahogany for the new beading.

2 Cut 45-degree mitres with a sharp utility knife at either end of the new cock beading. Glue it in place with PVA (white) glue and hold it with spring clips (see p.57).

3 Cut a piece of cock beading to replace the missing beading. Cut 45-degree mitres at both ends, then secure the piece as in step 2.

4 When the glue is dry, use a block plane to remove any excess wood so that the beading is flush with the side of the drawer.

5 As the cock beading will almost certainly have a rounded edge this can be first shaped using a small paring chisel and followed by papering with fine-grade sandpaper.

Above: *The new cock beading should be stained and polished to match the existing beading, with efforts made to match any light distressing on the original.*

Replacing drawer runners

The drawer runners on this drawer have been completely worn away in places. Further damage has been done by the carcass drawer stops, which have grooved trenches into the drawer bottom (see p.60). The damaged runners must be removed and replaced with new ones.

MATERIALS AND EQUIPMENT
- flat-bladed knife
- hammer
- smoothing plane
- beech or mahogany
- tenon saw
- PVA (white) glue
- snap clamps
- toothbrush
- plane
- chisel

1 If the runners are glued to the sides and bottom, tap a flat-bladed knife slid between the runner and the side to break the joint.

2 Remove the damaged runners from the bottom by sliding the knife underneath and gently tapping it with the hammer.

3 Use the iron from a smoothing plane to remove any traces of old and perished glue.

4 Choose a similar wood to the old runners (usually beech or mahogany) and cut some runners to the same width and length as the old ones, but deeper to allow for planing at a later stage. Glue them into place.

5 Hold the new runners firmly in place with snap clamps and leave to dry. Remove any excess glue using a toothbrush and water.

6 This drawer also had runners attached to the exterior of the drawer sides, and these too had become worn. Remove and replace these with new ones, as before, gluing them to the replacement bottom runners.

◁ **7** When dry, plane the runners to the correct depth to enable the drawer to sit evenly in the carcass. This is very much a case of trial and error, but take care not to plane the runners too thin, or the drawer will sit unevenly.

▷ **8** The final touch is to cut an angled mitre at the back of each runner. This will help the drawer to run smoothly as well as preventing snagging.

Replacing drawer runners...continued

◁ **9** Use a sharp chisel to cut a bevel at the back of each mitred runner. This will make removing the drawer and inserting it back into the carcass much easier.

Right: *With its new runners in place, the drawer will slide smoothly and freely.*

Replacing drawer stops

Drawer stops are designed to prevent a drawer from sliding in too far, and ensure that all the drawers line up correctly when closed. Stops are normally fitted so that they come into contact with the back of the drawer front, although they may be placed at the back of the drawer. If the runners wear, the stops may also become worn. In this case, the stops had worn away to expose their fixing nails, which had gouged the drawer bottoms.

1 Using a flat-bladed knife and a hammer, gently tap the knife between the worn stops and the carcass, and lift the stops away.

2 When the stops have been removed, they may leave behind the fixing nails. Remove these with a pair of pincers.

3 Insert one of the drawers into the carcass. Pulling the drawer forward slightly, measure the gap between the drawer bottom and the carcass. Cut a block of wood to a thickness that will be less than this measurement, to ensure that it does not interfere with the smooth running of the drawer, then cut it into two squares of suitable size. Repeat for the other drawers.

4 Glue the new drawer stops to the carcass, setting them slightly forward of the original positions. Before the glue has dried, insert both drawers, carefully aligning them with the front of the chest. This will push the blocks into their correct positions. Leave the glue to dry completely before removing the drawers. If extra strength is required, drive a few pins (tacks) through the stops.

MATERIALS AND EQUIPMENT
- flat-bladed knife
- hammer
- pincers
- tenon saw
- wood blocks
- PVA (white) glue
- pins (tacks)

Cutting a dovetail joint

The dovetail joint was one of the most common types of joint used in the construction of furniture in the 18th and 19th centuries. In the main, it was used when two flat sections overlapped each other and a strong, secure joint was required, such as in carcass, plinth, drawer and cornice construction. Small dovetails can be difficult to cut, and the skill of the cabinet-maker is demonstrated by the quality of his dovetails.

This drawer, which dates from 1780, has lost one of its sides, but fortunately the interior parts used to house the ink bottles have survived. Before work starts, the drawer must be dismantled by gently tapping it apart using a cabinet hammer and a block of protective hardwood. The drawer dovetails are finer than normal so care must be taken not to damage them during the dismantling process. The drawer was made from

Cuban mahogany, and a piece of matching wood must be found for the new side. Once the new dovetail joints have been cut, the drawer can be reassembled.

MATERIALS AND EQUIPMENT
- Cuban mahogany
- tenon saw
- marking gauge
- utility knife
- fine dovetail saw
- G-clamp
- clamping blocks
- chisel
- mallet
- hammer
- hardwood blocks
- mortise gauge
- narrow chisel or router
- PVA (white) glue

1 Dismantle the drawer. Find a matching piece of mahogany for the new side. If the colour is slightly different, it can be stained to match at a later stage, but it is important that the grain is the same. Cut it to the same size as the existing drawer side.

2 Measure the length of the dovetail pins on the existing drawer side, then mark them out on both ends of the new side using a marking gauge.

3 Hold the front of the drawer against the corresponding end of the new side, and transfer the pin lines with a utility knife. Repeat with the back, holding it against the other end of the new side.

4 Place the side in a vice with the marked lines held vertical. Using a fine dovetail saw, cut along the waste side of the marked lines. This will help to achieve good tight joints.

▷

Cutting a dovetail joint...continued

5 Clamp the side to a flat piece of wood and use a sharp chisel and a mallet to cut halfway through the top of the waste wood. Turn the side over and cut through from the other side. This will ensure a clean cut.

6 Some drawer bottoms are nailed in place, but this one is housed in a groove. Mark this groove on the new side with a mortise gauge set to the thickness of the bottom.

7 Cut the new groove for the drawer bottom with a narrow chisel or a router.

8 Tap the dovetail joint gently together with a small hammer and a hardwood block. The joint should be tight with no gaps. If necessary, make small adjustments by paring the wood with a utility knife.

Left: *The drawer can now be reassembled and the internal parts glued back into place.*

Cutting a dovetail housing

1 *Lay the newly cut dovetail pins against the end grain of the corresponding piece of wood. Mark the outline of the pins clearly with a utility knife.*

2 *Measure the depth of the pins with a marking gauge, then score a line across wood. Use a dovetail saw to cut on the waste side of the marked lines for a good fit, using the scored line as a depth guide.*

3 *Bring the two parts of the joint together. It should be tight with no gaps. Apply a small amount of glue, then remake the joint. Before it sets, check that the drawer is square by using gauge sticks.*

Repairing a split drawer bottom

During the 18th and 19th centuries, drawer bottoms were made up from a number of pieces. They were then either slotted into grooved drawer sides or nailed flush. Due to the fact that wood will shrink across its grain, it is not uncommon to find that the original glue line has come away with the shrinkage of the various sections of a drawer bottom, leaving gaps. This drawer has an unsightly gap, so the bottom must be removed and the gap reglued before the drawer can be reassembled.

MATERIALS AND EQUIPMENT
- chalk
- stiff-bladed knife
- hammer
- smoothing plane
- PVA (white) glue
- sash clamps
- clamping blocks
- nails
- cloth (cotton rag)

1 Mark the underside of the various pieces of the drawer bottom with chalk before removing them. This shows which way around the boards should be and also how the parts join together.

2 The bottom slides into grooves on the drawer sides but is nailed to the drawer back, and the nails have been punched below the surface. To remove them, insert a stiff-bladed knife between the wood and the back, then tap it with a hammer to cut through the nails.

3 Remove the bottom pieces and clean off the old glue with the iron from a smoothing plane. Replace the bottom pieces in the correct order, applying a small amount of PVA (white) glue along the glue lines.

4 Clamp the bottom pieces together with a sash clamp and clamping blocks, and nail the back piece to the drawer back at the same time. Finally, wipe off any excess glue and chalk marks with a cloth (cotton rag).

Right: *Once restored, the drawer bottom will be gap-free, giving an aesthetically more pleasing appearance.*

REPAIRING DOORS

The doors in pieces of furniture can suffer from a number of problems, some of which are easier than others to put right. Broken glass is common in glazed doors, while doors of all types can stick in their openings or become distorted.

As with most other types of furniture, any carved detail or mouldings may be damaged over the years, while the hardware (hinges, catches and locks) can also give trouble.

Repairing a glazed door

From the late 17th century onward, glass was introduced into furniture construction. It was hand blown and rolled into very thin sheets. During the 18th and 19th centuries, the style of the glazing bars, or astragals, found in bookcase and cabinet doors varied greatly, but the actual method of securing the glass remained fairly constant.

This door is from a mid-18th-century bookcase. One of the smaller panes has been cracked and so needs to be replaced. Once the glass has been removed, a new pane must be inserted. This will be held in place with plaster rather than putty. Once dry, the plaster can be stained to match the original putty. There are various sources for suitable glass (see Selecting glass, p.66).

MATERIALS AND EQUIPMENT		
• iron	• felt-tipped pen	knife
• chisel	• diamond-tipped	• fine brush
• glass	glass cutter	• water-based
• methylated	• steel	stain
spirits (methyl	straightedge	
alcohol)	• plaster	
• fine wire (steel)	• ochre	
wool	• flat-bladed	

1 First, remove the original mid-18th century putty. Do this by heating the putty with an iron to soften it.

2 When the putty is soft, begin to pare it away with a sharp chisel.

3 Remove all the old putty from the back of the astragal with the chisel, making sure not to cut into the wood supports, since this would weaken the construction of the door.

◁ **4** When the putty has been removed, carefully lift out the broken pieces of glass (you may wish to wear protective gloves for this job). If the glass is antique and hand blown, do not discard any pieces of a reasonable size, but store them carefully for a possible later use.

▷ **5** Period hand-blown glass was often not flat but uneven in texture, so it was bedded on to a putty base to counter any movement. This was the case in this door, so pare away the bedding putty as well.

6 Clean your selected piece of glass using methylated spirits (methyl alcohol) and fine wire (steel) wool, and check that it matches the existing glass in both colour and type.

7 Place the glass over the astragal and mark out the shape with a felt-tipped pen.

8 Using a diamond-tipped glass cutter, scribe along the marked line and cut the glass to size and shape.

◁ **9** Putty was used to hold the original glass in this door, and you could use putty to fix the new pane, but it takes several days to harden fully. A better choice is plaster, which hardens in minutes and can be pre-coloured. Mix the plaster with a small quantity of ochre before stirring in the water.

10 The glass will not be completely flat, so apply a small layer of plaster with a flat-bladed knife to act as a levelling base. ▷

Replacing a glazed door...continued

11 Press the glass gently into position on the wet plaster.

12 Apply more plaster with a flat-bladed knife and shape it into a bevel.

13 While the plaster is still malleable, trim away the excess with a sharp chisel.

14 When the plaster is dry, stain it with a water-based stain mixed to match the colour of the original putty.

15 Finally, apply a darker stain on top of the coloured plaster to try to mimic the patina of the original putty. This should blend the repaired glazed panel to match the others.

Right: *As the restored pane is of a matching glass and was fitted properly, it is indetectable from the original when viewed from the exterior.*

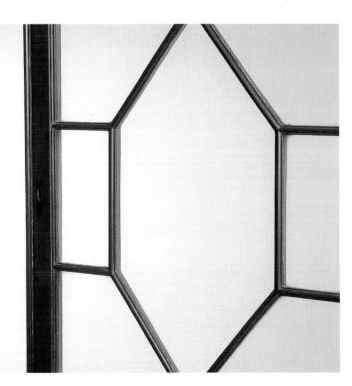

Selecting glass

It is always preferable to use an old piece of glass to replace glass lost from antique furniture, as new glass will stand out. While certain specialist glass manufacturers still supply old-style glass, the best sources are old picture frames and stocks collected from previous repairs, which can be cut down to the required size.

Repairing a sliding tambour

Sliding tambours were introduced in the 18th century. Their construction method is simple: lengths of wood are bonded to a cloth backing, which can be slid back and forth around a curve.

Several lengths of wood have become loose on this 18th-century Dutch cabinet, and closer inspection revealed that a previous repair was causing the problem. The tambour must be detached from the cabinet, the pieces of wood removed from the old backing and reglued to a new linen cloth.

MATERIALS AND EQUIPMENT
- masking tape
- flat-bladed knife
- long-shanked screwdriver
- smoothing plane
- Irish linen
- PVA (white) glue

1 The tambour is held in place only through tension, so, once the frieze at the top has been removed, pulling the top of the frieze should release it. Alternatively, the back of the cabinet may have to be removed.

2 Lay the tambour face up on a flat surface. Secure the lengths of wood with 5cm/2in strips of masking tape, laid at right angles to the strips, at 10cm/4in intervals.

3 Turn the tambour over. Lift up a corner of the backing material with a flat-bladed knife, then pull it away and discard it.

4 Some metal strips from an earlier repair were revealed. These would have held the tambour together, but would have been too stiff to allow it to run freely. Use a long-shanked screwdriver to remove these strips. Scrape away any remains of glue with the iron from a smoothing plane.

5 Cut a piece of Irish linen to match the height and width of the tambour. Coat the back of the tambour with glue, then smooth the linen over the surface, making sure that there are no air bubbles or wrinkles. Leave to dry. Remove the masking tape and test the flexibility of the tambour by manipulating it into a curved shape, then refit it.

Above: *The restored sliding tambour, with its decorative parquetry frieze replaced, now operates smoothly in the cabinet.*

Refitting a door

The door on this 18th-century wall cupboard has dropped due to wear on the pin hinge. This has resulted in the door no longer sitting square in the frame, and a gap can be seen at the top. The two alternatives are to have the hinge remade or to pack up the bottom of the door, which is an easier and quicker method.

MATERIALS AND EQUIPMENT
- flat-bladed knife
- fine brush
- hammer
- stain
- tenon saw
- wood
- hand drill

1 Due to the construction of the cabinet, the hinges have been attached with hand-made clout nails rather than screws. Ease the nails out gently by tapping a flat-bladed knife in behind the hinge.

2 Fold the detached part of the hinge forward to reveal the housing. Cut a thin packing piece of wood to size and trim to fit in the recess of the housing. This will counteract the dropping of the hinge.

Left: *With the packing piece in place and the hinge replaced, the door once again sits squarely in its frame.*

3 Drill pilot holes into the packing piece (see p.77). These will make sure that the original clout nails, which will be weakened by their age, will not shear off when they are refitted. Stain the packing piece to match the surrounding wood.

Correcting a minor twist

Doors come in many styles and designs, but one theme that is common to all doors is that they can warp, twist or bind due to climatic change. In extreme cases, the door may need to be completely remade, with the core wood being replaced. In most cases, however, there are a number of steps that can be taken to help alleviate the problem. The door on this mid-18th-century bookcase has twisted slightly and no longer closes flush against the opposite door. Since the problem is fairly minimal, a technique known as half and half (half packing/half paring) will be employed to correct the twist.

MATERIALS AND EQUIPMENT
- screwdriver
- chisel
- tenon saw
- wood
- hand drill
- wood drill bit

1 Unscrew both hinges from the carcass and remove the bookcase door. Keep the original screws safely.

2 Cut a small packing piece of wood to fit in the bottom hinge recess. This will push the bottom of the door out slightly. Drill pilot holes for the screws and refit the hinge.

◁ **3** Pare down the top hinge recess slightly then refit the hinge. This will pull the top part of the door nearer to being flush with the opposite side. Both the packing and paring have an element of trial and error about them, so make small changes at a time and refit the door regularly to make sure that a correct balance is obtained. Note that the packed and pared areas do not need staining because they are completely covered by the refitted hinges.

Right: *With the corrective work undertaken, the door is once again able to close flush against the opposite side.*

PROJECT: 19TH-CENTURY DESK

When this desk was originally purchased, its age was unknown. It was not immediately apparent, therefore, whether or not it was worth carrying out restoration. After some investigation and upon close examination, however, it was discovered to be a 19th-century English oak-veneered writing desk, and, despite the generally distressed condition of the piece, it was indeed worth restoring to its former glory.

ASSESSING THE PROJECT

The desk is damaged in several areas, particularly the top, the drawers and the carcass, with areas of veneer missing in some places. An initial assessment was made of each problem in order to decide in which order to proceed. The final decision was to split the restoration work into three sections – first the top, then the drawers and finally the carcass – after which the whole desk would be polished and cleaned.

The top
• split wood
• torn and worn leather

The carcass
• damage to frame supports
• splits to pedestal
• missing veneer on plinth corners

The drawers
• damaged runners
• missing knobs

Repairing the desk top

The wood of the desk top needs extensive restoration, but the leather is too badly damaged to be saved and so must be replaced. The first stage is to secure the splits in the wood from underneath using butterfly keys. Then the splits in the top surface should be filled, planed and polished, and finally some new leather applied.

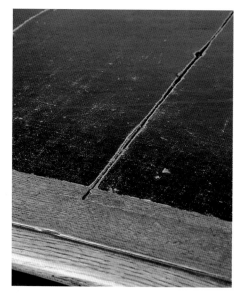

SECURING THE SPLITS

Although the splits in the desk top appear dramatic, they require one of the more straightforward repairs, using softwood butterfly keys that are inset and glued underneath the top at right angles to the split. These keys secure the split and so prevent any further movement.

MATERIALS AND EQUIPMENT

- screwdriver
- long pole
- G-clamp
- clamping block
- toothing plane
- cardboard
- softwood
- tenon saw
- utility knife
- router
- chisel
- PVA (white) glue
- jack plane
- fine brush
- water-based stain or ochre

1 Remove the top drawers and lift the desk top and frame off the pedestals. Prise a corner of the leather free and wrap it around a long pole. Pull the leather gently away while rolling the pole toward you.

2 Remove the second piece of leather in the same way. As the leather is removed, you can assess the extent of the damage to the top. In this case, the splits in the top go right through the wood.

3 Secure the top to the workbench with a G-clamp and clamping block, then run a toothing plane over the wood to remove any old glue or pieces of leather.

4 To clean the edges, remove the iron from the toothing plane and scrape it along the surface, parallel to the polished edge, until no traces of old glue or leather remain.

5 Remove the clamp and turn the top over. In this instance, a previous owner had tried, unsuccessfully, to restore the desk top by screwing a wooden panel over the split. This has to be removed.

6 Detach the frame from the top by removing the recessed screws, known as pocket screws, with a screwdriver. This will provide complete access to the desk top. Set the frame aside for later repairs. ▷

Securing the splits ...continued

7 Make a cardboard template for the butterfly keys (see right). Mark out as many keys as you need on a piece of softwood and cut them out with a tenon saw.

Butterfly keys

Butterfly keys are dovetail-shaped blocks of wood that are inset at right-angles to a split, thus preventing the split from opening up further. They should be made from a softwood, such as pine, and their size and number depend upon the size of the split and the depth of the wood. In the case of a split that cannot be closed up, the keys will secure the surface in its current position. If the split can be glued and clamped, the keys will secure the glued join.

8 Place a butterfly key over one end of the first split, about 13cm/5in from the edge of the desk top, with the waist of the key directly over the split. Mark out the position of the key with a utility knife.

9 Cut an angled back chamfer around the key outline with the utility knife. This will prevent the edge from splintering when it is routed.

10 Set the depth stop on a router to slightly less than the thickness of the key, then cut out the marked key shape.

11 Use a sharp chisel to straighten the edges of the cuts. It is important to match the recess exactly to the shape of the key to ensure a snug fit. Continue cutting shapes at 23cm/9in intervals along all the splits.

12 Apply a thin coat of glue to each recess and press in a key. When they are dry, plane the keys level with the surface of the desk top using a jack plane.

13 Use a water-based stain or ochre that matches the colour of the wood to tint the keys. Although the underside of the desk top will not be seen, this is a finishing touch that should always be made.

PREPARING THE TOP

Any cracks or dents in the upper surface of the desk top will show through the leather, as the construction of the desk top made it simply impossible to glue the top together. Therefore, they must be filled and the top smoothed down. A two-part wood filler can be applied to smaller cracks, but larger splits also require filling with thin strips of wood. The veneer around the edge of the upper surface requires some patching, and must be cleaned and polished before the leather is applied.

MATERIALS AND EQUIPMENT

- softwood
- tenon saw
- PVA (white) glue
- hammer
- chisel
- two-part wood filler
- putty knife
- smoothing plane
- veneer patch
- fine wire (steel) wool
- methylated spirits (methyl alcohol)
- rubber
- polish

1 Cut strips of softwood to the correct width and length to fit the larger splits snugly. Apply a generous amount of PVA (white) glue to the splits.

2 Put each sliver of wood over its split and set it in place by lightly tapping it down with a hammer. Wipe away the excess. Leave to dry.

3 Use a sharp chisel to pare away any excess wood. Continue until each insert is flush with the desk top.

4 Apply a two-part wood filler to all cracks and knot holes with a putty knife, packing the filler in well. Leave to dry.

5 Plane the surface with a smoothing plane to smooth off the filler and to produce a surface to which the leather can adhere.

6 Patch the damaged areas of veneer banding on the edge of the top, making sure the grain and figure match (see p.81). ▷

Preparing the top...continued

7 Lightly rub the veneered edge with fine wire (steel) wool to remove any top wax and loose dirt. Always work in the direction of the grain, otherwise you will leave scratches.

8 Moisten the wire wool with methylated spirits (methyl alcohol) and lightly rub the veneered edge again. This will give a surface to which the new polish can adhere.

9 Charge a rubber with polish and apply a layer to the veneered edge to enhance the grain and colour of the veneer. A final polish will be applied when the desk is reassembled.

LEATHERING THE TOP

The value of the desk demands that a best-quality piece of hide should be selected and purchased from a tannery. Prior to cutting it, examine it for scars, scratches and stretch marks, all of which will be emphasized when coloured and polished (see p.34). Time taken at this stage will ensure that the finished result complements the rest of the restoration work undertaken.

MATERIALS AND EQUIPMENT

- large brush
- PVA (white) glue
- leather
- "bone"
- utility knife
- cloths (cotton rags)
- leather sealant
- water-based stain
- tooling wheel
- pressurized spray gun
- cellulose lacquer
- dividers
- roll of gold leaf
- steel rule
- decorative pattern wheel
- stamp
- wax (optional)

1 Spread PVA (white) glue evenly over the wood, making sure it covers the whole area, especially up to the edges. Lay the new piece of leather down on the desk top, making sure it covers the whole area.

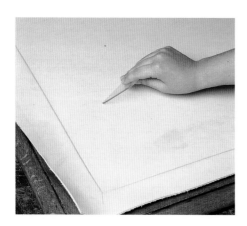

2 With the aid of a tool known as a "bone", flatten out any blisters and uneven areas, working from the centre outward. Use the edge of the "bone" to make sure the leather is pushed into the corners (see p.34).

3 Use a sharp utility knife to cut away the excess leather, taking care that the cut is accurate and no gaps are left. Use the edge of the veneer banding as a cutting guide.

4 When the leather is dry, wipe the surface with a leather sealant, applied with a cloth (cotton rag). This will make sure that the leather dyes will give an even covering and not become blotchy.

5 Apply a water-based stain with a cloth in a circular motion and gradually build the colour to the desired intensity. Avoid the veneer banding around the edge.

6 Heat a tooling wheel to create a decorative border. Apply even pressure and, once the wheel is rolling, do not stop until you reach the end of the leather.

7 With the leather fitted, coloured and sealed, the next stage is to lacquer it. To make sure the lacquer will not mark the veneer, mask it off (wrap it) with paper.

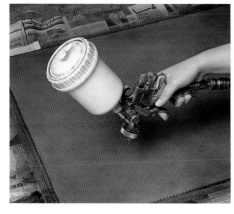

8 Using a pressurized spray gun, apply an even coat of cellulose lacquer. If necessary, apply a second coat once the first has dried. Lacquering gives a protective layer to the leather as well as locking in the colour and stopping it bleeding out.

9 When the lacquer has dried, and the paper has been removed, decide on a decorative border. There are many styles and patterns to choose from, but it is a good idea to seek advice on what would be suitable. Use dividers to decide the best proportions.

10 Lay a roll of gold leaf in place and put a steel rule on top, then run the tooling wheel along the leaf. Keep the pressure even and ensure the wheel is at spitting heat: if too hot, it will burn through the gilt, and if too cold, the gilt will not stick to the leather.

11 Apply a more decorative pattern wheel inset inside the original single line, working freehand. Carefully peel the gold leaf away.

12 Join the corners using a stamp, which again has been heated to spitting heat. This gives a neat appearance and completes the process. The top can now be sealed with a coat of wax or another thin layer of lacquer.

13 Finally, using a utility knife, carefully lift off any excess areas of gilt and tidy up the finish. Obtaining a perfectly straight and even line, like many restoration techniques, takes many years of practice.

▷

Repairing the drawers

All the drawers are suffering from worn runners, which cause the drawers to sit unevenly and to stick. Two of the drawers are also missing knobs, which need replacing, and there are several patches of chipped and missing veneer to be restored.

REPLACING THE RUNNERS

Drawer runners are often attached to the drawer bottoms, and are designed to allow the drawer to run smoothly and evenly in the carcass. In this case they are attached to the drawer sides, so the drawer will have to be dismantled before work can begin. Remove the plinths first; these will be repaired at a later stage.

MATERIALS AND EQUIPMENT
- masking tape
- marker pen
- stiff-bladed knife
- hammer
- hardwood block
- circular saw
- mahogany
- PVA (white) glue
- snap clamps
- flat piece of wood
- plane
- gauge sticks
- small pins (tacks)
- G-clamps

1 Remove the drawers from the pedestals and place them on the workbench. Label each part of each drawer in a way that identifies not only which drawer it belongs to but also its position within that drawer.

2 Starting with the first drawer, slide the bottom out of the frame. You may need to remove small pins in order to be able to do this (see p.63, step 2). Put the drawer bottom to one side.

3 Stand the drawer up and place a hardwood block on the inside of one of the sides. Gently knock the block with a hammer until the dovetail joints loosen and the pieces come apart.

4 Using a circular saw with the fence set, cut a small amount from the drawer runner. This is to provide a parallel edge for the new wood to attach to. Note that the guard has been removed for the photograph.

5 Cut a straight strip of matching mahogany to the same length as, but marginally deeper than, the drawer side and glue it to the freshly cut edge of the runner. Apply snap clamps and leave to dry.

6 Place a flat length of wood between the drawer side and the workbench, then clamp them both securely to the bench. Plane the edge of the runner flush with the drawer side. Repeat steps 2–6 for all the other worn drawer runners.

7 Now all the drawers can be reassembled. Apply only a small amount of PVA (white) glue to the inside of the dovetails on the drawer backs and fronts, as the tightness of the joints will hold them together.

8 Immediately after applying the glue, tap the dovetail joints together using a hammer and a block of wood. Apply only light pressure to avoid unnecessary damage to the delicate dovetail pins.

9 Use gauge sticks to check that each drawer is square. Do this straight after gluing, so any minor adjustments can be made.

10 When the glue has set, slide each of the drawer bottoms back in place, and secure them with three or four small pins (tacks).

Pre-drilling a nail hole

When hammering a small pin (tack) or clout nail into a hardwood, you may find that it can bend or shear off. An easy remedy is to pre-drill the hole at a slightly smaller diameter than the nail (a pilot hole).

◁ **11** Clamp a hardwood block at the back of the workbench to keep each drawer securely in place, then plane the runners so that they fit into the desk and run smoothly.

▷

REPLACING THE KNOBS

The desk retains its original oak wooden knobs, although a number have become detached and are now missing. Using an original as a template (pattern), copies must be turned to match.

MATERIALS AND EQUIPMENT
- callipers
- oak
- lathe
- turning tools
- paring tool
- dividers
- skew chisel
- very fine-grade sandpaper
- spirit-based (alcohol-based) stain
- fine brush
- rubber
- polish

1 Take a measurement from an original knob using a pair of callipers, and use this to determine the diameter of the new knob. Prepare a piece of oak for the lathe, then turn it to the correct diameter.

2 Mark out the depth of the knob using a paring tool, then remove it from the lathe and pare it away from the rest of the wood. Replace the knob into a lathe chuck.

3 Turn the shape of the wooden knob, constantly comparing its shape and size to the original using dividers.

4 With the proportions determined, turn the final shape, using a skew chisel to create the domed shape of the knob.

5 Finish off the knob by lightly sanding it while it is still rotating in the lathe. Take care during this process that you do not alter the shape of the knob.

◁ **6** The completed replacement knob should be identical to the original. Repeat this procedure to make as many knobs as are needed. Stain and polish them to match the other knobs, before fitting them in place.

Repairing the carcass

The drawer runners have worn deep grooves in the frame; one of the pedestals has a large split in the back due to shrinkage; and both plinths are missing sections of veneer and have sustained damage to the core wood. The frame supports for the drawer runners will be repaired with new pieces of wood, while the split will be glued and clamped. Damaged core wood on the plinths will be replaced and the veneer patched.

MATERIALS AND EQUIPMENT

- screwdriver or pincers
- hardwood block
- hammer
- circular saw
- softwood
- PVA (white) glue
- jack plane
- sash clamps
- clamping blocks
- nails

REPAIRING THE DRAWER SUPPORTS

The action of opening and shutting the top drawers over many years has resulted in deep grooves being worn into the frame supports. This damage must be repaired, as otherwise the frame will continue to be worn away until it breaks in two.

1 Place the frame on the workbench and remove the screw or nail that secures each end of a support to the frame. Place a piece of hardwood over the support and gently knock the support out using blows from a hammer.

2 Make two parallel cuts down the centre with a circular saw. Reset the saw and turn the support on to its side. Making sure the depth is set correctly, run the support over the saw to remove the worn parts. Note that the guard should always be in place.

3 Using the circular saw, cut two fillets of softwood to replace the worn parts of wood that have been removed, and glue them into position.

◁ **5** Glue the restored frame supports back into position and clamp until dry. Hammer nails into each end while the supports are still firmly clamped.

4 Plane the new wood flush with the original. The inserts will allow the replaced drawer runners to run on a level surface. Repeat for the other damaged support.

▷

REPAIRING THE PEDESTAL

Shrinkage has caused a crack to develop from the top to the bottom of the back panel of one of the pedestals. The panel is attached to the sides by dovetail joints, which have been veneered over. To leave the dovetails and veneer intact, the back is scribed down each side and only the broken sections removed. Once the crack is repaired, the split is glued and clamped in place and a fillet is added to fill the gap.

MATERIALS AND EQUIPMENT

- marking gauge
- circular saw
- stiff-bladed knife
- hammer
- iron
- oak
- PVA (white) glue
- sash clamps
- G-clamps
- clamping blocks
- plane
- nails
- veneer

1 Place the pedestal on the workbench and scribe along both edges of the back with a marking gauge. Cut along the lines with a circular saw to free the broken sections.

2 Cut through the fastening rails with a stiff-bladed knife and hammer, then prise the broken sections off the pedestal. Turn the pedestal on to its front.

3 Remove the thin strip of veneer left between the right-hand edge and the scribing line by placing a hot iron on it to soften the glue and prising it away.

◁ **4** Before mending the split, cut a fillet of oak to compensate for the back being narrower now than it was. Apply glue to both sides of the split and also to the fillet, and glue this to the right-hand edge of the back. Clamp the pieces together, using sash and G-clamps and clamping blocks. Leave to dry.

5 Trim the fillet and plane it to the correct width. Glue the new back into place and nail it at top and bottom. Apply a strip of veneer to cover the fillet and bare edge.

RESTORING DAMAGED WOOD AND VENEER

Sections of veneer are missing from the corners of the plinths, after years of being kicked and knocked, and the core wood on to which the veneer was laid is also damaged. The core wood needs to be rebuilt, and the veneer patched and polished to restore the piece. This is a relatively straightforward task but it is important that the new core wood is cut and fitted correctly before the more cosmetic veneer can be applied.

MATERIALS AND EQUIPMENT

- snap clamp
- set (carpenter's) square
- utility knife
- router
- wood
- tenon saw
- bench hook
- PVA (white) glue
- masking tape
- small block plane
- veneer
- scotch glue
- cabinet scraper
- fine-grade sandpaper
- sanding block

◁ **1** Place one of the plinths on the workbench. Clamp it firmly to the bench using a snap clamp, or fix it into the vice.

▷ **2** Score a line close to one of the damaged sections of veneer and core wood, using a set (carpenter's) square and a utility knife.

3 Cut away the damaged area of core wood with a router. Repeat this procedure on each of the damaged corners, removing the wood and veneer if necessary, or just the veneer if the core wood is undamaged.

4 Cut replacement pieces of core wood from a suitable wood using a tenon saw and bench hook.

▷

81

Restoring damaged wood and veneer...continued

5 Glue the replacement patches into place using PVA (white) glue.

6 Apply strips of masking tape, pulled tight, to secure each patch as it sets. Make sure that all the edges are square, to achieve a firm joint.

7 Plane each new section of wood with a small block plane. Continue until there is enough depth to allow for a replacement piece of veneer.

8 Select a piece of oak veneer that matches the original. Cut it to size. Apply scotch glue to the new wood and tape the veneer firmly into place. Leave to dry.

9 Using a cabinet scraper, level the veneer patch to match the original veneer. Trim off any excess using a sharp utility knife.

10 Sand the veneer with fine-grade sandpaper and a sanding block. Repeat steps 1–10 for the other plinth.

11 Note the importance of choosing new wood that matches the original grain of the existing veneer.

Reassembling and polishing

With all the carcass repairs completed and the surface cleaned and revived, the desk can now be reassembled. This will involve replacing the knobs after they have been coloured and stained to match the originals, and may include servicing the locks.

MATERIALS AND EQUIPMENT
- screwdriver
- brush
- stain
- ground pumice
- soft cloth (rag)
- polish

1 Reattach the plinths to the pedestals using the original screws. If you have carefully labelled the fittings when the carcass was dismantled you can ensure that they are put back on the right pedestal.

2 Stain any replacement veneer or moulding to match the original finish before polishing.

3 After filling the grain with ground pumice and polish, polish the new patches of wood until they match the rest of the desk.

Left: The restored and reassembled desk is ready once again to be used. Treated with care, it should not need further attention for several generations.

PROJECT: GRANDFATHER CLOCK

The longcase, or, as it is more commonly known, the grandfather clock, was a familiar part of home furnishings during the mid-18th and 19th centuries. Although they were commissioned during the late 17th and early 18th centuries, their use became more widespread after 1800.

They came in various shapes, styles and sizes, and by the mid-19th century the cases were often made of the finest veneers by master cabinet-makers. Like all furniture, however, they can suffer the ravages of time, as is the case with this example.

ASSESSING THE PROJECT

This longcase contains an illustrated mahogany clock. The clock is in good working order, but the case is damaged in several areas and requires new mouldings to be made, loose ones replacing, as well as general repairs to the carcass. The veneer, which has good colour and patination, needs patching and blisters putting down. Finally, a missing roundel on the hood will need to be replaced and the surface revived, polished and waxed.

The hood
- loose and missing veneer
- missing pediment roundel and core wood
- missing inner slip

Tip

The clock workings are in good order. Prior to work on the case, the workings should be carefully removed and stored in a dry, dust free environment until the clock is ready for reassembly.

The trunk and plinth
- missing and blistered veneer
- loose and missing mouldings

Repairing the hood

The decorative scrolls on the pediment of a longcase are easily damaged when the clock is moved. In this instance, veneer has been damaged, some of the long-grain moulding is loose or has been lost, some groundwork is missing and a roundel has been lost. Finally, an inner slip by the hood door is missing and needs to be replaced.

SECURING VENEER AND RESTORING THE CORE

Much of the loose veneer can simply be removed, reglued and clamped. It is best to remove large areas, rather than cut through the veneer with a knife, but if the veneer is in danger of breaking, score a line with a sharp utility knife to make sure of a straight edge. Before starting work, the hood must be removed and placed on a workbench and the works should be removed and carefully stored.

MATERIALS AND EQUIPMENT
- flat-bladed knife
- smoothing plane
- softwood
- tenon saw
- PVA (white) glue
- paper
- G-clamps
- jigsaw (saber saw)
- snap clamps
- lengths of wood
- spokeshave
- utility knife
- Cuban mahogany
- veneer

◁ **1** Gently prise away both pieces of loose moulding, and then the veneer (which came away in two pieces), with a flat-bladed knife. Put the pieces of moulding and veneer to one side.

▷ **2** Scrape the core wood with the iron from a smoothing plane to remove any traces of old glue. Cut a softwood clamping block to fit the shape of the area that is to be re-veneered.

3 Apply PVA (white) glue to the hood and put the pieces of old veneer back in place, matching the edges as exactly as possible.

4 Place a piece of paper and the clamping block on top of the relaid veneer. Apply G-clamps and leave to dry. Repeat steps 1–4 for all the remaining loose veneer.

5 Place a piece of softwood behind the swan-neck moulding that is missing its core, and trace around the moulding. Cut out this shape with a jigsaw (saber saw). ▷

Securing veneer and restoring the core...continued

6 Glue the softwood shape to the back of the pediment, then clamp it in place using snap clamps braced against lengths of wood. When the glue has dried, remove the clamps and shape the core with a spokeshave.

7 One of the inner slips is missing on the door of the hood. Cut a piece of Cuban mahogany to size, secure it in place with a small G-clamp, then mark the mitre with a utility knife.

8 Secure the new piece of wood in place by gluing veneer patches on to the back. This is a good way of joining two pieces of wood together when there is only a small area of joint between them.

TURNING AND ATTACHING A ROUNDEL

One of the roundels on the pediment is missing and needs to be replaced. This is done by using a faceplate on a lathe, which allows a flat surface to be turned to the required size and profile. The original remaining roundel can be removed to act as a template (pattern).

MATERIALS AND EQUIPMENT

- faceplate
- tenon saw
- wood
- steel rule
- jigsaw (saber saw)
- screws
- screwdriver
- flat-bladed knife
- mahogany
- PVA (white) glue
- paper
- G-clamp
- lathe
- dividers
- parting gauge
- skew chisel
- hammer
- spring clips

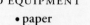

1 Choose a faceplate of a suitable size for the new roundel. Cut a square piece of wood and mark its centre point. Lay the faceplate on the wood and mark out its circumference.

2 Cut the circumference out with a jigsaw (saber saw), then screw the faceplate to the wood. Use a flat-bladed knife to remove the original roundel from the hood, so that it can be used as a template (pattern).

3 Glue the selected piece of mahogany from which the roundel will be turned on to the wooden side of the faceplate. Placing paper with glue on either side between the wood blocks will aid removal at the end of turning.

4 Screw the faceplate on to the end of the lathe and put the lathe rest in place.

5 Measure the circumference of the original roundel with dividers, then, with the lathe turning, transfer this to the new wood.

6 Use a parting gauge to turn the roundel to the correct diameter. Make sure that the sides are at right angles to the front.

7 When the correct size has been obtained, turn the shape of the face with a skew chisel. Keep checking the shape against the original roundel.

8 When the correct size and shape have been achieved, hold a handful of shavings, removed earlier, lightly against the turning while it is spinning to give a smooth finish.

9 When finished, the roundel should be exactly like the original. Remove it from the faceplate by tapping a flat-bladed knife between the paper–glue joint.

10 Both roundels can now be glued into place on the restored hood, along with the two areas of missing moulding, and held with spring clips while the glue sets.

Restoring the trunk and plinth

While the trunk is in fairly good order, there are some mouldings that need to be replaced, some blisters to put down and some damaged areas of veneer to be patched. These are all typical of the types of damage that you would expect to find on any period carcass or trunk furniture.

MATERIALS AND EQUIPMENT
- block of MDF (medium density fiberboard)
- iron
- paper
- clamping blocks
- G-clamps
- cloth (cotton rag)
- flat-bladed knife
- veneer
- circular saw
- utility knife
- PVA (white) glue

REPAIRING AND REPLACING VENEER

Some pieces of veneer can be reglued, but others are missing, so some old pieces of veneer must be sourced. Whenever possible, reuse all veneer that is removed from the clock elsewhere on the longcase. For example, one of the cross-banded lengths was missing several pieces, so the remaining pieces were used as patches for other areas, while a new strip was fitted to replace the whole length.

▷

Repairing and replacing veneer...continued

1 Put any blisters down with a hot block. The heat generated from the previously heated block will soften the glue underneath the veneer. Clamping the veneer will rebind it to the core as it cools.

2 Place a damp cloth on the remaining veneer of the most damaged cross-banded length. Place a hot iron on the cloth to loosen the glue. Remove the veneer by lifting it with a flat-bladed knife.

3 Select a closely matching section of veneer. It is vital to match colour, figure and patination as closely as possible, and it is here that the importance of a well-stocked breaker store (see p.26) can be seen.

◁ **4** In this instance, cut the veneer away from its backing with a circular saw rather than steaming it off. This is to make sure that the surface is not marked and retains its original surface. Make sure that this replacement veneer is cut to match the thickness of the existing veneer.

▷ **5** Cut mitres at the ends of the veneer length to match the existing veneer corners, and then, after trimming it to fit with a utility knife, glue the veneer into position with PVA (white) glue. Clamp until dry.

6 Use the veneer previously removed to patch the less-damaged length, trimming the damaged areas first to ensure good joints.

7 When completed, and if the grain is carefully matched, the joints should be barely visible.

REPLACING AND RESTORING MOULDINGS

Loose mouldings need to be refixed, missing cock beading replaced and damaged areas patched.

MATERIALS AND EQUIPMENT

- toothbrush
- wood
- tenon saw
- PVA (white) glue
- chisels
- fine-grade sandpaper
- G-clamps
- clamping blocks
- jack plane
- flat-bladed knife
- smoothing plane

◁ **1** There are a number of missing pieces of moulding on the trunk. Clean away all traces of the old glue with a toothbrush, then cut a new piece of matching wood to size and glue it into position with PVA (white) glue.

2 Using a sharp paring chisel, round off the square edges to give the cock beading its standard rounded profile.

3 Smooth the moulding with fine-grade sandpaper, making sure not to mark the polished surfaces.

4 Patch any other areas of missing moulding and, with the aid of chisels or carving tools, flow in the new areas to follow the profile of the original.

◁ **5** Part of the plinth moulding is missing. Find a suitable piece of matching wood, plane it to match the original, then glue it to the base. Apply G-clamps and clamping blocks.

▷ **6** Remove very loose mouldings on the trunk of the clock with a flat-bladed knife.

▷

Replacing and restoring mouldings..continued

◁ **7** Remove any loose glue from the carcass and mouldings with the iron from a smoothing plane.

▷ **8** Reglue the mouldings. Due to their unusual shape, it is often necessary to cut clamping blocks to match the mouldings, so that an even pressure can be applied.

Polishing

Due to the excellent untouched colour of the mahogany veneer, the polishing was confined to colouring the repairs and lightly reviving the surface.

MATERIALS AND EQUIPMENT
- fine wire (steel) wool
- fine brush
- stain
- rubber
- polish
- cloth (cotton rag)
- wax
- mutton cloth

◁ **1** After all the restorations have been completed, give the polished surface a light dusting with fine wire (steel) wool. The aim is to remove any loose dirt and wax but not to damage the patinated surface.

2 Stain all the repairs, then charge a rubber with polish and apply a thin layer to revive the surface of the clock (see pp.49–50). As the majority of repairs to the surface were carried out using old surface veneers, this is more a case of reviving than repolishing the surface.

3 When the polish has hardened, cut it back with fine wire wool, wax it, then finally buff it with a soft mutton cloth.

Setting up the clock

A clock, with its precision movement, must be perfectly level to work properly. When you have chosen a suitable position, level the case, using a spirit level to check, and then screw it to the wall to give it stability. Add the pendulum and weights, and, if balanced correctly, the clock should begin to work once you start off the pendulum. If the clock does not keep good time or keeps stopping, seek the advice of a qualified clock-restorer unless you know what you are doing. Remember that all grandfather clocks should be cleaned and oiled by a qualified clock-restorer every ten years.

MATERIALS AND EQUIPMENT
• spirit level
• screws
• screwdriver
• coins

1 After levelling and screwing the clock case in place, sit the works on top of the trunk. The seat board, to which the works are attached, must be perfectly level; use coins to help to achieve this.

2 With the clock screwed into position, and the works in place, replace the hood and fit the door if necessary (the majority of clocks have a door already fixed to the hood).

Right: *The clock, now restored and in place, will need no further attention for several years, other than being wound up once a week.*

GLOSSARY

animal glue Also known as scotch glue and used from the 17th century onwards.

astragals Glazing bars on cabinet furniture, forming a geometric pattern.

bain-marie A pot containing hot water in which another container, holding animal glue, gesso or bole, for example, can be gently heated.

banding Decorative inlays of veneer that are used for aesthetic effect. They can be either long-grained or cross-grained and on earlier pieces can be joined to give a chevron effect, known as herringbone.

blooming The name given to the white marks left on a polished surface that has been water-damaged or chilled.

bole A clay-like substance that is used in the gilding process.

boulle Also known as buhl, this is the use of fine brass inlay inset into tortoiseshell or ebony backgrounds.

bracket foot A square foot which might have a shaped profile on the inside. The foot most commonly used during the 18th century.

breaker A piece or a collection of pieces of furniture used in the restoration of another item of furniture.

bun feet A ball type of foot favoured during the 17th century and replaced by the bracket foot in the 18th century.

butterfly key A butterfly-shaped piece of wood used to secure and hold splits. It is inset into a piece so that the grain runs at right angles to the main wood. Also known as a dovetail key.

carcass The actual framework of a piece of furniture. Depending on the period, this is either solid or veneered.

cascamite A glue used when forming laminates or shape work. It is very strong but also brittle.

cock beading Thin strips of decorative beading often found around drawer fronts.

colour The tone or shade that wood develops over time.

conservation To maintain a piece by undertaking as little work as possible so as not to alter its present or original form (*see* restoration).

core The moulded shape on to which veneer or mouldings are applied.

cornice The top of a carcass piece of furniture often decorated with dental mouldings, cross bandings or a pediment.

cross-grain mouldings Wood applied to a softwood backing and planed to a moulded profile, applied to a carcass for aesthetic reasons. Introduced during the 17th century, they are more decorative than long-grain mouldings.

Cuban mahogany Mahogany imported from Cuba during the 18th and 19th centuries and the preferred wood for quality furniture. It is densely grained and red in tone when first polished.

cutting gauge A tool fitted with a small blade that is used across the grain to cut a groove. Often used prior to fitting boxwood lines.

de-nibbing The removal of dust that has combined with polish to form small raised nibs on a surface after polishing. This is done by lightly using fine wire wool in the direction of the grain. The surface is then waxed.

dental mouldings Small rectangular pieces applied to a cornice and resembling square teeth. Popular during the mid-18th century.

dovetail saw A fine-bladed saw used for cutting accurate and delicate dovetails.

escutcheon The brassware used in conjunction with locks for both aesthetic and protective reasons.

fading/fad Filling the grain in wood with a mixture of polish and pumice powder. The cloth with which it is applied is known as a fad.

fire gilding A mixture of gold and mercury applied to a metal base and heated until the mercury evaporates and binds the gold to the metal. Favoured during the 18th century; used on the mounts and handles of the finest pieces.

French curve A kidney-shaped scraper used on concave curves.

French polishing Using shellac polish, which is usually applied with a linen and wadding (batting) rubber.

fret A lattice-like decoration, in which open fret is pierced and blind fret is applied to a solid background.

gauge sticks Two lengths of stick which are held together and used to check the equal diagonal measure of a frame to ensure it is square.

gesso A plaster-like substance that is used in the gilding process.

graining Using surface stains and colours to mimic the grain of a solid piece of wood. Favoured during the early 19th century.

Honduras mahogany Mahogany imported from Honduras during the 18th and 19th centuries and favoured for carcass construction.

kickers Strips of wood applied to the inside carcass of a chest, running along the top of the drawer linings, to stop the drawers tipping forward when extended.

linings The name given to the sides and often the bottom of a drawer.

long-grain mouldings Mouldings planed from one length of wood along the grain and applied to a carcass for aesthetic or structural reasons.

marquetry Inlays of decorative scenes.

marriage Two parts of a piece of furniture that started life separately but have now been brought together. Such an example would be a bureau bookcase in which both halves started life with another part.

mortise The hollow housing part of a mortise and tenon joint, the most widely used joint in furniture construction.

mortise gauge A marking tool that has a small steel point and is used along the grain to mark the shoulders of a mortise.
overloe A shaped block used in conjunction with sandpaper.
parquetry Inlays of geometric patterns.
patera A round or oval, raised decoration often found on cornices or the tops of legs. Can also be used in veneer form.
patination This refers to the build up of waxes, natural greases and dust that over numerous years combines to form a desirable finish on a surface.
pediment Found on top of a carcass and, depending on the period, can be arched, broken-arched or swan-necked in shape.
piecrust The shape of a top, usually applying to a tripod table. It looks like the top of a pinched pastry pie top.
plinth The platform base on which a carcass will sit.
PVA glue Polyvinylacetate glue, also known as white glue. Ideal for daily use.
reeded decoration A raised decoration of parallel, tapering lines, usually found on chair and table legs.
reeds Raised dome-shaped decoration applied along the length of a surface.
restoration Work to return a piece as near as possible to its original form but retaining its integrity (*see* conservation).

revive a surface The action of attending to any minor damage or surface oxidation of a polished surface while not repolishing the whole top.
rubber Wadding (batting) wrapped in linen, which is used to apply shellac.
runners The strips of wood attached to the bottom or sides of a drawer on which the drawer will run. Sometimes also found as part of the carcass.
skiver Leather taken from sheep. Not as good quality as cow hide.
splay feet A shaped bracket foot that is splayed in profile. Favoured during the late 18th century.

spring clip A workshop-made cramping device made from upholstery springs. Ideal for securing awkward shapes.
stringing Thin lines of inlay, usually of ebony or box, which were used for both aesthetic reasons and as protective edges.
tenon The protruding part of a mortise and tenon joint, which is the most widely used joint in furniture construction.
twist When wood bows in two directions.
warp When a piece of wood has bowed along its length or width.

FURTHER INFORMATION

British Antique Furniture Restorers' Association (BAFRA)
The Old Rectory
Warmwell, Dorchester
Dorset DT2 8HQ
UK
Tel/fax: 01305 854822
Email: headoffice@bafra.org.uk
Web: www.bafra.org.uk

British Antique Dealers' Association (BADA)
20 Rutland Gate
London SW7 1BD
UK
Tel: 020 7589 4128
Fax: 020 7581 9083
Web: www.bada.org

Association of Art and Antique Dealers' (LAPADA)
535 Kings Road
Chelsea
London SW10 0SZ
UK
Tel: 020 7823 3511
Fax: 020 7823 3522
Web: www.lapada.co.uk

Association of Restorers
8 Medford Place
New Hartford
NY 13413
USA
Tel: (315) 733–1952
Fax: (315) 724–7231
Web: www.assoc-restorers.com

Art and Antique Dealers' League of America, Inc. (AADLA)
1040 Madison Avenue
New York
NY 10021
USA
Tel: (212) 879–7558
Fax: (212) 772–7197
www.artantiquedealersleague.com

The National Antique & Art Dealers Association of America, Inc.
220 East 57th Street
New York
NY 10022
USA
Tel: (212) 826–9707
Fax: (212) 832–9493

Australian Antique Dealers' Association
PO Box 24
Malvern
Victoria 3144
Australia
Tel: (03) 9576 2275
Fax: (03) 9576 2106
Email: secaada@ozemail.com.au

PICTURE CREDITS

INDEX

W.J. COOK & SONS

W.J.Cook & Sons was established by Bill Cook in 1962. His reputation for outstanding work quickly spread and since those early days clients have included the British Royal Household and Government, museums, leading collectors, dealers and private individuals. While still retaining a London workshop, the business is based in Marlborough, Wiltshire. With the cabinet-making, machine and polishing shops it is a business that is recognized as one of the leaders in its field. After training at the London College of Furniture, three of Bill's sons joined the business and have helped develop and further expand its range and facilities. Now their own children are being encouraged to pick up the tools with a view to taking the family tradition to a third generation.

The services carried out are many and include cabinet-making, gilding, carving, polishing, lock repairs, leathering and upholstery. Being a true family business it means that every restoration commission is undertaken with great care. With over 40 years of experience at the very highest level, together with an extensive in-house

library and access to furniture archives, any restoration carried out is authentic in every detail.

Virtually all the restoration work is still carried out using 18th- and 19th-century tools: their band saw was used in the construction of the panelling for the *Queen Mary*.

A final note: antique furniture if badly restored can rarely be returned to its original glory. Therefore, it is important that a suitably qualified restorer should be consulted when necessary.

Left: from left to right, Bill, Stephen, Richard, Billy and (seated) Catherine Cook.

High Trees House
Savernake Forest
Marlborough
Wiltshire
SN8 4NE
01672 513017
william.cook@virgin.net
www.wjcookandsons.com

167 Battersea High Street
London
SW11 3JS
020 7736 5329

Author's acknowledgements

When approached to write this book we were delighted to accept. For a number of years we have been acutely aware of the absence of any book that was written and extensively photographed in a commercial restoration workshop and which showed and explained clearly how various techniques are carried out on a day to day basis. Drawing from over 40 years of experience and a lifetime's collection of materials and tools, we hope to have given the reader an authoritative insight into the subject.

While the overwhelming majority of work was undertaken "in house", there are grateful thanks due to others who have been invaluable in their help both with advice and in the use of their facilities: Barry Ansell of R.D. Robins Ltd, London, on upholstery; Geoff Collier of Colliers Castings, Hooe, on casting methods; Les Crispin of Capital Crispin Veneer, London, on veneers, Alan Dallison on leathers, Bob Dunn of A. Dunn & Son, Chelmsford, on marquetry; and Optimum Brasses, Tiverton, on brassware.

Special thanks go to the staff in our workshops for making sure that the work needed for this book was always ready on time. A big thank you goes to Paul Lyon for his sterling work, without which this book would have been impossible.

On a personal note, like all family businesses, an unsung hero is our mother Catherine who has always been there keeping the wheels turning. Thanks also to my brothers Richard and Stephen with whom it is very much a team effort, and not to forget Justin, who has chosen to follow his own path.

Thanks to all those who have been encouraging and supportive throughout the whole process of writing this book, including Richard my life-long friend, for his humour, often dispensed from across the world, Nathalie, whose words of wisdom, while not always fully appreciated are always carefully considered, and my three sons William, Henry and James, for just being themselves.

Finally this book is for my father from his sons, and for our sons and daughters from their fathers in the hope that they may one day take the business onwards for another generation.

BILLY COOK